NAJC

NATIONAL GEOGRAPHIC KIDS

ULTIMATE Explorer
FIELD GUIDE

Wildflowers

Libby Romero

NATIONAL GEOGRAPHIC
WASHINGTON, D.C.

Contents

JACK-IN-THE-PULPIT p. 18

FAIRY SLIPPER p. 30

TALL THIMBLEWEED p. 47

FIELD PANSY p. 58

About Wildflowers

SILVERY LUPINE p. 86

LOOK ALONG THE HIGHWAY in springtime and you're likely to see colorful wildflowers. Wildflowers are angiosperms (seed-producing flowering plants) that grow in natural places. As their name indicates, wildflowers are not cultivated plants. They grow on their own in the wild without the help of people.

WHAT'S THE STORY?

Everywhere you look, you can see flowering plants. It's no wonder, because angiosperms are the most abundant and diverse type of plant on Earth. About 80 percent of all plants are angiosperms.

Despite their dominance, angiosperms are relative newcomers on Earth. Fossil records show that they appeared suddenly about 130 million years ago. That may seem like they've been around a long time. But geologically speaking, they haven't. Nonflowering plants had already been growing for more than 200 million years.

Once angiosperms appeared, they spread quickly. Scientists think this happened because the plants had a short life cycle. They could start to grow in new ground and evolve faster than their competitors could.

As a result, angiosperms quickly evolved into a spectacular variety of plants. Today, their ranks include everything from herbs and vines to shrubs and giant trees. They also include wildflowers.

WHY DO PLANTS HAVE FLOWERS?

Flowers are usually the showiest parts of a plant. There's a reason for that. Flowers attract insects and other animals. When these guests visit, they move pollen from one flower to another. This is how the plants reproduce. How do the flowers attract these pollinators?

- **Color:** Butterflies and birds like red. Bees prefer blue and yellow. These pollinators visit brightly colored flowers in the daytime. Moths and bats fly at night. The flowers they pollinate are white. This makes them easy to see in the dark. Some flowers even have ultraviolet color patterns that are invisible to the human eye. Pollinators can see these patterns. They also see other colors differently from the way we do. That's because pollinators' eyes don't have the same color receptors as human eyes.

- **Smell:** Some flowers smell sweet. Others smell like rotting flesh. Each smell attracts the specific pollinator that particular plant needs to reproduce. Pollinators have a much more sensitive sense of smell than we do. They can detect floral fragrances at great distances. They can even tell apart flowers that we may think smell the same.

To keep pollinators interested, the flowers must offer a reward. This reward comes in the form of pollen and nectar. As the pollinators feast, the plants reproduce.

HOW WILDFLOWERS GROW

A wildflower begins its life as a seed. When conditions are just right, the seed sprouts, or germinates. The embryo inside the seed grows into a seedling.

Wildflowers also have the same basic parts as many other plants. Roots hold the plant in the ground and absorb water and minerals from the soil. The stem supports the plant. It also provides a system for water and nutrients to travel from the roots to other parts of the plant. The leaves capture sunlight so the plant can make food.

When the plant matures, it produces flowers. Flowers attract pollinators. They move pollen from the male part of one flower to the female part of another. Pollen can now grow to reach the ovary, where eggs are fertilized and grow into new seeds. In some plants, the ovary grows into a fruit (think of an apple). It protects the seeds. Soon the seeds spread and grow into new plants.

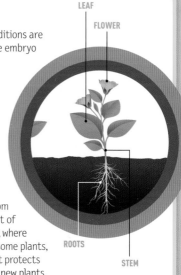

LEAF
FLOWER
ROOTS
STEM

EACH PART OF A PLANT HAS A SPECIFIC JOB.

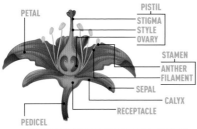

PETAL
PISTIL
STIGMA
STYLE
OVARY
STAMEN
ANTHER
FILAMENT
SEPAL
CALYX
RECEPTACLE
PEDICEL

FLOWERS CONTAIN THE MALE AND FEMALE PARTS THAT PLANTS NEED TO REPRODUCE.

THE PARTS OF A FLOWER

Flowers come in all shapes and sizes. Even so, every flower has the parts it needs to reproduce. These parts include:

petal: individual segment of the corolla, typically colored

stamen: male part of a flower

anther: part of the stamen that makes and stores pollen

filament: slender support for the anther

sepal: individual segment of the calyx, usually green and leaflike

receptacle: enlarged area bearing flower organs

pedicel: stalk bearing the flower

pistil: female part of the flower

stigma: part of the pistil that receives pollen during pollination

style: connecting stalk between stigma and ovary

ovary: base of the pistil, containing one or more eggs

corolla: the structure formed by petals, which often contains nectar at its base

calyx: the structure formed by sepals; typically encloses the corolla

A World of Wildflowers

Wildflowers are all around you. Most are herbaceous plants, meaning they have nonwoody stems. All are angiosperms, or plants that produce flowers. But the size and shape of the flowers can vary greatly.

Some flowers are so small that you barely notice them. Others are large and showy. And the blooms on some wildflowers have such a short life span that people recognize the plant more by its leaves than by its flowers.

There are up to 400,000 different species of angiosperms. As with all other living things, scientists sort angiosperms into groups based on their common traits. By studying the genetic makeup of plants, scientists discovered that one of the most important features of a plant is the structure of its pollen. Because of that, scientists divide angiosperms into several groups.

The two largest groups of angiosperms are monocots and eudicots. Monocots have pollen with one pore. A eudicot's pollen has three pores. Monocots have a more direct link to the first angiosperms. But eudicots are more common. About 75 percent of all angiosperms fall into this group.

There are other basic differences between monocots and eudicots, including:

- Monocots have one cotyledon, or first leaf. Eudicots have two.

- Monocots' flower parts come in threes. Most eudicots have flower parts in multiples of four or five.

- The veins in a monocot's leaves run parallel to one another. Eudicot leaves have a network of veins. To see the difference, look at a blade of grass. Then look at a dandelion's leaves.

- The bundles of veins in a monocot's stem are scattered. In a eudicot, these bundles form a ring.

Despite their differences, both kinds of plants produce a wide variety of flowers.

SCIENTIFIC CLASSIFICATION OF THE BLACK-EYED SUSAN

Scientists have classified wildflowers and all other plants into groups with common features or properties. Check out the complete classification of the Black-eyed Susan.

Kingdom	Plantae (plants)
Subkingdom	Tracheobionta (vascular plants)
Superdivision	Spermatophyta (seed plants)
Division	Magnoliophyta (flowering plants)
Class	Magnoliopsida (eudicots)
Subclass	Asteridae
Order	Asterales
Family	Asteraceae (asters)
Genus	*Rudbeckia* L. (coneflower)
Species	*hirta* (Black-eyed Susan)

Scientists typically refer to a wildflower by its genus and species names, or *Rudbeckia hirta* L., because sometimes common names can be confusing. Two very different kinds of wildflowers can share a common name.

Where to Find Them

In most places, if you look around, you will spot wildflowers. They dot the sides of roadways. They fill valleys with color. Wildflowers blossom in deserts and on mountaintops. They even float on top of water.

Like all plants, wildflowers have certain requirements to grow. Experts have done a lot of research to identify the conditions different types of plants need to survive. The result of all that work is the U.S. Department of Agriculture (USDA) Hardiness Zone Map.

This map breaks North America down into growing zones. Each zone is 10°F warmer (or colder) on average than the zone next to it. It also takes into account elevation, how far it is to a large body of water, and even whether a place is on a hill or in a valley. If you're searching for a certain kind of wildflower, look up its growing zones in the map below.

Average annual minimum temperature (°F)

Zone 0 Below -60
Zone 1 -60 to -50
Zone 2 -50 to -40
Zone 3 -40 to -30
Zone 4 -30 to -20
Zone 5 -20 to -10
Zone 6 -10 to 0
Zone 7 0 to 10
Zone 8 10 to 20
Zone 9 20 to 30
Zone 10 30 to 40
Zone 11 40 to 50
Zone 12 50 to 60
Zone 13 60 to 70

ALASKA (U.S.)

CANADA

UNITED STATES

HAWAII (U.S.)

Map is based on the USDA Plant Hardiness Zone Map and the Plant Hardiness Zones of Canada map courtesy of the Canadian Forest Service.

TAKE A HIKE

The next step is to go outdoors. Wildflowers are every-where! Look for sunny, open areas. Most wildflowers require a lot of sunshine to grow. You can search along beaches, in the woods, in a vacant lot, in your backyard, or in a park. Look along streambeds and in wet ditches. You might even spot a Fragrant Water Lily floating on a pond!

FRAGRANT WATER LILY p. 15

WHEN TO FIND THEM

The wildflower season begins in early spring, but it continues all year long. What you see will mostly depend on when you visit a particular location.

For example, the Great Smoky Mountains National Park is famous for its wide array of wildflowers that bloom throughout the year. There are more than 1,500 kinds of flowering plants here.

If you visit the park in early spring, you may spot Spring Beauties or Bloodroot. Then come the trilliums, violets, and bluets. By May many of the early spring blossoms begin to fade, and summer flowers take over. By late summer and throughout the fall, sunflowers, goldenrod, and asters appear.

PLAYING IT SAFE

Look for these Danger! signs throughout this guide to know if a wildflower could harm you. The Buffalobur Nightshade, for example, has a pretty yellow flower. But the plant is covered with dense, stiff, sharp spines. This is one to look at but never touch!

SPIKE

Some plants are toxic. Giant Hogweed is covered with a toxic sap. All you have to do is brush against the plant to be exposed to it.

POISON

Some plants are only toxic if eaten. Eating locoweed causes strange behavior, impaired vision, and sometimes death. Spotted Water Hemlock, found throughout North America, is one of the most toxic plants. Every part of the plant is poisonous.

SPOTTED WATER HEMLOCK p. 135

The best way to stay safe when observing wild-flowers is to be prepared. Wear protective clothing. Use insect repellent and wear sunscreen. Avoid wearing scented products that might attract insects. If you are allergic to pollinators, such as bees, always carry an emergency epinephrine kit.

Protecting Wildflowers

Everyone loves to pick wildflowers. Collecting them is a beautiful way to remember a special day. But what seems like a harmless act can have far-reaching consequences.

Wildflowers are a vital part of the ecosystem. Pollinators—including insects, birds, beetles, and bats—depend on nectar and pollen from wildflowers for food. The seeds that grow as a result of pollination are food for birds, insects, and many small mammals. If wildflowers disappear, so does the food source for these animals.

To protect species, people can plant wildflowers to create new habitats, such as a butterfly garden. An inexpensive way to start a butterfly garden is to plant from seeds.

You should also get to know the plants in your own backyard. Many of the plants you see are native species. Others have been introduced and become invasive, meaning they've taken over the environment. Removing invasive plants helps native wildflowers survive.

Finally, you can remind adults not to use chemicals in places where native wildflowers grow. Some wildflowers are weeds and people use pesticides to control them. Unfortunately, non-target wildflowers can be affected, too.

✓ CHECKLIST FOR FINDING WILDFLOWERS IN THE FIELD

The best way to learn about life cycles, pollinators, flowers, and seeds is to go out and take a look. Here are some things to bring on your search for wildflowers:

✓ HAND LENS OR MAGNIFYING GLASS

Wildflowers come in many sizes. But even the biggest wildflowers have some parts that are hard to see with the naked eye. A magnifier will help you get a closer look.

✓ A GUIDE

Take this book with you on hikes, bike rides, and car trips. See how many wildflower species in the book you can identify. You also might want to get a more focused guide that includes all the species in your area.

✓ A NOTEBOOK

Pack a small notebook and pen or pencil in your backpack. You'll want to keep a record of the species you see and when and where you find them. You can even make quick sketches that will help you identify them later.

✓ PROPER CLOTHING

Many insects—including some that you'd prefer to avoid—are attracted to bright colors. Wearing earth colors like tans and greens helps you blend into your surroundings. Long pants, long sleeves, and sturdy shoes will protect against poison ivy and ticks. Wear a hat for sun protection.

HOW TO USE This Book

ALTHOUGH WHAT YOU SEE WILL VARY WITH LOCATION AND TIME OF YEAR, wildflowers are everywhere. Take this book with you on your hunt to help you locate and identify wildflowers you see.

CALIFORNIA POPPY p. 42

Wildflower Entry

THIS IS WHERE YOU'LL FIND THE WILDFLOWER'S COMMON NAME.

HERE IS THE WILDFLOWER'S SCIENTIFIC NAME, ITS ORDER, ITS AVERAGE HEIGHT (NOT THE WORLD RECORD), THE HABITATS IT GROWS IN, WHERE IT'S FOUND IN NORTH AMERICA, THE HARDINESS ZONES IT GROWS IN, THE TYPE OF PLANT (ANNUAL, BIENNIAL, OR PERENNIAL), AND WHETHER IT'S A MONOCOT OR A EUDICOT.

THIS TEXT GIVES GENERAL INFORMATION ABOUT THE SPECIES, INCLUDING LIGHT AND MOISTURE REQUIREMENTS, BLOOM TIME, AND BLOOM COLOR.

DISCOVER A FUN FACT OR INTERESTING DETAIL ABOUT THIS SPECIES.

QUICKLY IDENTIFY A WILDFLOWER BY LOOKING FOR THESE BASIC FEATURES. CAN YOU NAME THE CORRECT SPECIES IN 10 SECONDS?

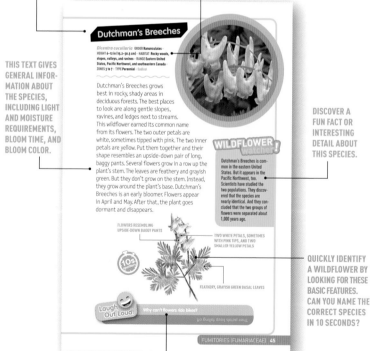

Dutchman's Breeches

Dicentra cucullaria · ORDER **Ranunculales** · HEIGHT **6–12 in (15.2–30.5 cm)** · HABITAT **Rocky woods, slopes, valleys, and ravines** · RANGE **Eastern United States, Pacific Northwest, and southeastern Canada** · ZONES **3 to 7** · TYPE **Perennial** · Eudicot

Dutchman's Breeches grows best in rocky, shady areas in deciduous forests. The best places to look are along gentle slopes, ravines, and ledges next to streams. This wildflower earned its common name from its flowers. The two outer petals are white, sometimes tipped with pink. The two inner petals are yellow. Put them together and their shape resembles an upside-down pair of long, baggy pants. Several flowers grow in a row up the plant's stem. The leaves are feathery and grayish green. But they don't grow on the stem. Instead, they grow around the plant's base. Dutchman's Breeches is an early bloomer. Flowers appear in April and May. After that, the plant goes dormant and disappears.

WILDFLOWER watcher!

Dutchman's Breeches is common in the eastern United States. But it appears in the Pacific Northwest, too. Scientists have studied the two populations. They discovered that the species are nearly identical. And they concluded that the two groups of flowers were separated about 1,000 years ago.

FLOWERS RESEMBLING UPSIDE-DOWN BAGGY PANTS

TWO WHITE PETALS, SOMETIMES WITH PINK TIPS, AND TWO SMALLER YELLOW PETALS

FEATHERY, GRAYISH GREEN BASAL LEAVES

Laugh Out Loud! Why can't flowers ride bikes?

Their petals keep falling off.

FUMITORIES (FUMARIACEAE) 45

WILDFLOWER JOKES, PUNS, AND RIDDLES WILL MAKE YOU AND YOUR FRIENDS LAUGH—ALTHOUGH SOME OF THE PUNS MIGHT MAKE YOU GROAN! TRY THEM ON YOUR FAMILY, TOO.

SPECIAL FEATURES CALLED WILDFLOWER REPORTS give you a closer look at wildflowers' appearance, their amazing adaptations, and their remarkable life cycles.

LEARN ABOUT THE DIFFERENT SPECIES THAT REPRESENT THE THEME OF THE REPORT.

A TEXT BLOCK GIVES GENERAL INFORMATION ABOUT SPECIAL FEATURES RELATED TO APPEARANCE, BEHAVIOR, OR LIFESTYLE.

A CAPTION DESCRIBES THE MAIN PHOTO.

Classification

Scientists describe and classify wildflowers, just as they do all other living things. Each type of wildflower is a species. Closely related species are grouped together in a genus, and each genus is grouped with relatives in a family. The wildflowers in each group share characteristics as well as common genes inherited from an ancestor. This is how each wildflower gets its scientific name. The scientific name is written in Latin and contains the wildflower's genus and species. Most also have a common name, or the name that nonscientists use. In many instances, one wildflower has different common names in different locations. To help you identify wildflowers, the common and scientific family names are found at the bottom margin of the pages. For wildflowers with several common names, one of the most widely used options is shown. For those with no common name, only the scientific name is given.

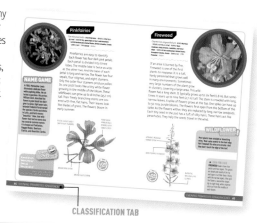

CLASSIFICATION TAB

AMBORELLA TRICHOPODA IS A RARE BASAL ANGIOSPERM
FOUND ONLY IN NEW CALEDONIA.

BASAL ANGIOSPERMS are the most primitive flowering plants. Most have woody stems, and they all produce flowers and seeds. Like monocots, their pollen has just one pore. And like eudicots, they tend to have a netlike pattern of veins in their leaves. These plants have characteristics of both monocots and eudicots. Yet they don't belong to either group. Basal angiosperms are found all over the world. Along with some wildflowers, they include trees, shrubs, vines, and aquatic plants. Fewer than 5 percent of all flowering plants are basal angiosperms. Check out these examples.

Fragrant Water Lily

The Fragrant Water Lily belongs to the Nymphaeales order of basal angiosperms. This aquatic plant has large, fragrant pink or white flowers and flat, round, floating leaves. It is found throughout North America.

Bay Starvine

The Bay Starvine is a perennial vine. It belongs to the Austrobaileyales order of basal angiosperms. It is found in the southeastern United States. In many places, it is an endangered species.

Virginia Snakeroot

The Virginia Snakeroot grows in the eastern United States. It is a Magnoliid, a large order of basal angiosperms. Native American tribes used this plant to make medicine for everything from worms to fevers. They even mixed it with saliva to treat snakebites.

Common Arrowhead

Sagittaria latifolia ORDER **Alismatales** · HEIGHT **Up to 4 ft (1.2 m)**
· HABITAT **Marshes, swamps, lakes, and ponds** · RANGE **Throughout North America** · ZONES **5 to 10** · TYPE **Perennial** · Monocot

This hardy aquatic plant grows in colonies along shorelines and in water that is 6 to 12 inches (15.2–30.5 cm) deep. Leaves growing above the water's surface are broad and shaped like arrowheads. That's how the Common Arrowhead got its name. Underwater leaves are much narrower. Between July and September, the Common Arrowhead produces one or two stalks. Each stalk has flowers that appear in spirals of three. Each flower has three white petals. By mid-fall, the plant begins to die back. It stores nutrients in golf ball–size tubers, or short, fleshy roots like potatoes that grow underground. These tubers are an important food source for waterfowl. That's why some people call them duck potatoes.

→ LOOK FOR THIS
COMMON ARROWHEADS have male and female flowers. To figure out a flower's gender, just look at its center. If the middle of the flower is bushy and yellow, it's male. If it contains a green mound, it's female.

WILDFLOWER watcher!

Water birds aren't the only ones that eat Common Arrowhead tubers. So do people. (They taste like potatoes!) Long ago, these tubers were an important part of Native American diets. Lewis and Clark ate them, too. Tubers were valuable enough to be used in trade.

BROAD ARROWHEAD-SHAPED LEAVES (ABOVE WATER)

CENTER OF FLOWER IS BUSHY AND YELLOW (MALE) OR A GREEN MOUND (FEMALE).

SPIRALS OF FLOWERS, EACH WITH THREE WHITE PETALS

ONE OR TWO STALKS

10s spotters

American Water-Plantain

Alisma subcordatum **ORDER Alismatales**
- **HEIGHT up to 3 ft (0.9 m)** - **HABITAT Shallow, slow-moving water and muddy bodies of water** - **RANGE Most of the United States and southeastern Canada** - **ZONES 3 to 7** - **TYPE Perennial** - Monocot

Riverbanks, pond shores, wet fields, and ditches are good places to spot the American Water-Plantain. This tall, spindly aquatic plant thrives in slow-moving water and muddy bottoms. It grows best in bright, sunny places. Flowers of the American Water-Plantain bloom between June and September. They are small, grow in spirals, and are usually white. But once in a while, the flowers may be pink. The American Water-Plantain's parts come in multiples of three. Each flower has three sepals, three petals, and six or more stamens. It has several pistils. The lower part of this plant grows underwater. Any leaves that form underwater quickly rot.

True or False

Native Americans made medicine out of the American Water-Plantain. True. Members of the Cherokee tribe used this plant to treat sores, wounds, bruises, swellings, ulcers, and upset bowels.

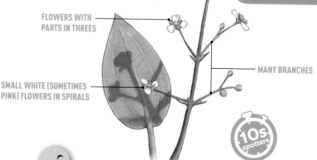

FLOWERS WITH PARTS IN THREES

MANY BRANCHES

SMALL WHITE (SOMETIMES PINK) FLOWERS IN SPIRALS

10s spotters

Laugh Out Loud! What's the most common name for a flower?

bud.

Jack-in-the-pulpit

Arisaema triphyllum ORDER **Alismatales**
◦ HEIGHT **1–3 ft (0.3–0.9 m)** ◦ HABITAT **Shady, wet woodlands** ◦ RANGE **Most of the United States and south-eastern Canada** ◦ ZONES **4 to 9** ◦ TYPE **Perennial** ◦ Monocot

The Jack-in-the-pulpit is a spring woodland wildflower. It gets its name from its flower, which has two parts. The Jack is a spike of tiny green to purple flowers. It's located inside the pulpit, a large, cylinder-shaped tube that folds over like a hood. Insects enter the flower through this hood. Male flowers have a hole in the bottom. So once insects are covered with pollen, they can head toward the light and escape. There is no escape route in a female flower. If an insect enters, it probably won't get out. But it will pollinate the female flowers if it has already visited a male plant!

DANGER!

If you see a Jack-in-the-pulpit, it's best to look but not touch. This plant's berries, leaves, and roots have a chemical in them that causes painful blisters.

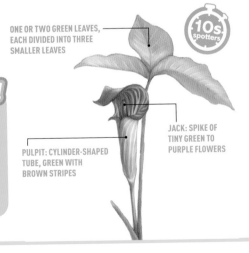

ONE OR TWO GREEN LEAVES, EACH DIVIDED INTO THREE SMALLER LEAVES

10s spotters

WILDFLOWER watcher!

You can grow a Jack-in-the-pulpit from a seed. It can take up to six years before you see the first flower, but then the plant starts to reproduce. It can also reproduce by spreading to form a colony. Each individual can live more than 25 years.

PULPIT: CYLINDER-SHAPED TUBE, GREEN WITH BROWN STRIPES

JACK: SPIKE OF TINY GREEN TO PURPLE FLOWERS

Skunk Cabbage

Symplocarpus foetidus ORDER **Alismatales**
◦ HEIGHT **1–3 ft (0.3–0.9 m)** ◦ HABITAT **Shady swamps
and muddy ground** ◦ RANGE **Northeastern United
States and southeastern Canada** ◦ ZONES **3 to 9**
◦ TYPE **Perennial** ◦ **Monocot**

The Skunk Cabbage is one of the first wildflowers to emerge in the spring. When it appears, it looks like a large, brownish purple-and-green speckled shell. Inside that shell is a cluster of tiny yellow flowers. Strangely, these flowers appear before any leaves do. They may even peek through the snow. There's no worry that they'll freeze, though. This plant's flowers can create their own heat. They can warm themselves up to about 59°F (15°C). The flowers melt the snow and ice around the plant! Soon the flowers wilt and the fruit containing seeds begins to develop. By late spring, fresh green leaves begin to appear. As they unroll, they turn dark green. Then the plant looks like a huge head of cabbage.

WILDFLOWER watcher!

Most of the time, a Skunk Cabbage has no odor. But its flowers produce a strong scent. If the leaves are bruised, they smell, too. And that odor is pretty awful. It reeks of decaying flesh. People may not like this smell, but it's a scent that certain pollinating insects can't resist!

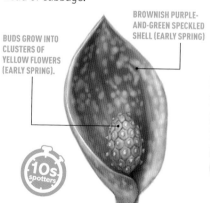

BROWNISH PURPLE-
AND-GREEN SPECKLED
SHELL (EARLY SPRING)

BUDS GROW INTO
CLUSTERS OF
YELLOW FLOWERS
(EARLY SPRING).

10s spotters

DANGER!

Unlike cabbage you can buy in the supermarket, the Skunk Cabbage is not edible. Many of its parts are poisonous. Eating this plant can cause your mouth and throat to swell. This can make it hard to breathe. An upset stomach can also occur.

Elegant Mariposa Lily

Calochortus elegans ○ ORDER **Liliales** ○ HEIGHT **2–8 in (5.1–20.3 cm)** ○ HABITAT **Grassy hillsides and open coniferous forests** ○ RANGE **Northwestern United States and California** ○ ZONES **3 to 6** ○ TYPE **Perennial** ○ **Monocot**

The Elegant Mariposa Lily has slender, bent stems; a few flowers; and just one grass-like leaf. That leaf is slightly taller than the flowers. The flowers form clusters around the stem. This plant grows from a bulb and blooms in May and June. Its flowers are white and have small purple spots in the middle. The blooms are very small. In fact, they're just one inch (2.5 cm) wide. They're also very hairy. People think the petals look like kittens' ears. That's why sometimes this plant is called Cat's Ears! To find an Elegant Mariposa Lily, you'll have to go to the mountains. They grow at mid to high elevations.

True or False

Another name for the Elegant Mariposa Lily is the Star Tulip.
True. This name refers to the starlike shape of the flower.

Europeans first saw the Elegant Mariposa Lily in the 1700s.
False. Lewis and Clark discovered this plant in the early 1800s. Their expedition was the first to record more than 300 plant and animal species for science.

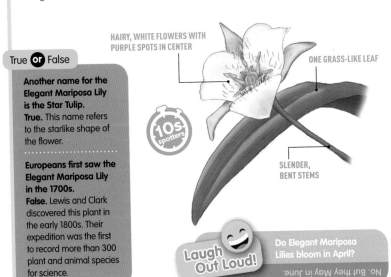

HAIRY, WHITE FLOWERS WITH PURPLE SPOTS IN CENTER

ONE GRASS-LIKE LEAF

10s spotters

SLENDER, BENT STEMS

Laugh Out Loud!

Do Elegant Mariposa Lilies bloom in April?

No. But they May in June.

Yellow Trout Lily

Erythronium americanum ORDER **Liliales** • HEIGHT **3–6 in (7.6–15.2 cm)** • HABITAT **Deciduous woodlands and openings** • RANGE **Eastern United States** • ZONES **3 to 8** • TYPE **Perennial** • Monocot

The Yellow Trout Lily got its name from its brown, spotted leaves. They look like the markings on fish called brown or brook trout. But this wildflower has other common names, too. For example, some people call it Adder's Tongue. That's because its leaves are shaped like tongues. Another name is Dogtooth Violet. Why? The bulb it grows from is shaped like a tooth. The flower itself is very pretty. It is yellow on the inside and bronze on the outside. The petals fold back toward the stalk. This makes it easy for bees to brush against the six brown stamens in the middle.

BRONZE ON THE OUTSIDE

SINGLE STALK

TWO, TONGUE-SHAPED LEAVES WITH BROWN SPOTS

DOWNWARD-FACING FLOWER THAT IS YELLOW ON THE INSIDE WITH SIX BROWN STAMEN

→ LOOK FOR THIS
YELLOW TROUT LILIES grow in colonies. If there's enough room, the plant produces a flower. If it's too crowded, it doesn't. Plants with flowers have two leaves. Plants without flowers have just one leaf.

Turk's-cap Lily

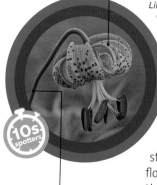

DROOPING ORANGE, SPOTTED REDDISH BROWN FLOWERS

SMOOTH, STOUT CENTRAL STEM

Lilium superbum ORDER **Liliales** • HEIGHT **4–6 ft (1.2–1.8 m)** • HABITAT **Wet meadows, swamps, and woods** • RANGE **Eastern United States** • ZONES **5 to 8** • TYPE **Perennial** • Monocot

The Turk's-cap Lily is the largest and most common lily in its range. People thought they looked like a cap that early Turks wore. Their flowers are dark orange at the tip and have reddish brown spots toward the middle. Right in the center, there's a bright green star. It's easy to see the star because the wildflower's petals and sepals curve back toward the stem. Because this plant is so large, it can produce up to 40 flowers. Each flower can be up to four inches (10.2 cm) wide.

A PAIR OR A SPIRAL OF LEAVES

Yellow Fritillary

Fritillaria pudica ORDER **Liliales** ∘ HEIGHT **1 ft (0.3 m)**
∘ HABITAT **Grasslands, sagebrush desert, ponderosa forests, mixed conifer forests** ∘ RANGE **Western United States and southwestern Canada**
∘ ZONES **3 to 7** ∘ TYPE **Perennial** ∘ Monocot

ONE HANGING BELL-SHAPED FLOWER THAT FADES TO PURPLE OR RUSTY RED

The Yellow Fritillary has a bright yellow flower that's shaped like a narrow, hanging bell. Each plant produces one flower. This wildflower begins its life as a bulb. It blooms from March to June. Toward the end of its bloom time, the Yellow Fritillary changes color. It becomes purplish or rusty red. Like many other plants, Yellow Fritillaries don't bloom every year. They may even take two years off. Instead of producing a flower during that time, the plant produces one broad, tongue-shaped leaf.

WILDFLOWER watcher!

Yellow Fritillaries don't like a crowd. They are usually found growing alone. At most, there will be two or three of these flowers grouped together.

HANGING BELL-SHAPED CREAM-COLORED FLOWERS WITH PURPLE SPOTS

Yellow Mandarin

Prosartes maculata ORDER **Liliales** ∘ HEIGHT **Up to 31.5 in (80 cm)**
∘ HABITAT **Moist wooded slopes** ∘ RANGE **Eastern United States** ∘ ZONES **5 to 8**
∘ TYPE **Perennial** ∘ Monocot

When the Yellow Mandarin first appears, it's not much to look at. It's just a single stalk covered with lots of curled-up leaves. As the leaves unfurl, the stem forks out into three branches. Then in April or May, the flowers appear. You can see them hanging down at the end of each branch. Finding Yellow Mandarins can be a bit difficult. These wildflowers aren't as common as they used to be. Plus, they tend to grow in rugged habitats that are hard to reach.

Laugh Out Loud!

Why didn't the flower feel unique?

It had a common name.

Largeflower Bellwort

Uvularia grandiflora ORDER **Liliales** ▪ HEIGHT **1–2 ft (0.3–0.6 m)** ▪ HABITAT **Rich, deciduous forests; thickets; floodplain forests** ▪ RANGE **Eastern United States and Canada** ▪ ZONES **4 to 9** ▪ TYPE **Perennial** ▪ **Monocot**

The Largeflower Bellwort has long, slender, yellow bell-shaped flowers. The tepals, which are a combination of the petals and sepals, curl around and twist. The plant's curly leaves are a very pale green. Most other plants have darker leaves. If you find one, it will probably look droopy. The weight of the flowers and leaves pulls the plant over. After the flowers die, lighter seed capsules take their place. The plant stands tall once again.

WILDFLOWER watcher!

Deer like to eat the leaves of the Largeflower Bellwort. When the deer population in an area increases, the number of these wildflowers in the woods goes down.

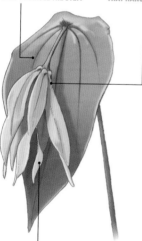

PALE GREEN, SPEAR-SHAPED LEAVES THAT ENCIRCLE THE STEM

PALE YELLOW, BELL-SHAPED FLOWER THAT HANGS FROM A PEDICLE

1–2 INCH (2.5–5 CM) TWISTED TEPALS

10S spotters

MAKE THIS!

Make a lily bouquet!

You will need: yellow and green paper; green and yellow pipe cleaners; scissors; pencil; tape

1. Fold and cut the yellow paper in half.
2. Across one end, cut six equal strips to make tepals. Stop cutting two inches from the edge.
3. Cut the corners off the tepals to make pointed tips.
4. Twist each tepal around a pencil to form loose cylinders.
5. Scrunch the bottoms of the tepals together.
6. Cut the yellow pipe cleaner into three equal pieces. Fold each piece in half.
7. Make a loop at the end of a green pipe cleaner. Secure the yellow pieces with the loop. Now you have six stamens and a stem.
8. Slide the green pipe cleaner down to the middle of the flower. Tape in place.
9. Cut leaves and tape them to the stem.

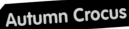
Autumn Crocus

Colchicum autumnale ORDER **Liliales**
∘ HEIGHT **3–6 in (7.6–15.2 cm)** ∘ HABITAT **Grassy meadows and damp woodland clearings** ∘ RANGE **Northeast, mid-Atlantic, and western United States**
∘ ZONES **4 to 8** ∘ TYPE **Perennial** ∘ Monocot

The Autumn Crocus is native to Europe. It was introduced to the United States as a fall-blooming ornamental flower. This plant is not related to crocuses that bloom in the spring. Those belong to the Iris family, and their flowers have three stamens and one style. The Autumn Crocus is a lily. Its flowers have six stamens and three styles. Only its leaves emerge in the spring. They die back in the summer. The flowers finally appear in August or September, growing on weak stems.

DANGER!

Never eat the Autumn Crocus. Every part of the plant is toxic, especially the bulbs and seeds.

WILDFLOWER watcher!

The toxins in the Autumn Crocus can kill you if you eat them. But they can also be put to good use. Researchers in England are using the plant to make a medicine called a "smart bomb" that targets cancer tumors. Other medicines for people and animals are made out of these toxins, too. They treat diseases like leukemia, gout, and some types of arthritis. Plants are the source of many medicinal products.

10s spotters

SIX STAMENS, THREE STYLES

WHITE TO LIGHT-PURPLE FLOWERS

Red Trillium

THREE DIAMOND-SHAPED LEAVES

ONE FLOWER WITH THREE DEEP RED PETALS

Trillium erectum ORDER **Liliales** · HEIGHT **6–18 in (15.2–45.7 cm)**
· HABITAT **Deciduous forests** · RANGE **Eastern United States and southeastern Canada**
· ZONES **4 to 7** · TYPE **Perennial** · Monocot

The Red Trillium has three diamond-shaped leaves on a tall, straight stem. Rising above the leaves is one downward-facing flower with three deep red petals. This species is sometimes called the Stinking Benjamin. That's because the flower gives off a foul odor. The stench has been compared to everything from pond water to a wet dog. Regardless, that odor does its job. It attracts flies that feed on dead animals, and the flies pollinate the flower. In some places, these flowers are endangered.

ONE LARGE WHITE WAXY FLOWER THAT TURNS PINK

Large-flowered White Trillium

Trillium grandiflorum ORDER **Liliales** · HEIGHT **12–18 in (30.5–45.7 cm)**
· HABITAT **Rich, mixed forests; thickets; swamps** · RANGE **Eastern United States and southeastern Canada** · ZONES **4 to 8** · TYPE **Perennial** · Monocot

The Large-flowered White Trillium is the largest and showiest species of trillium. This plant has a stout stem with three large oval leaves. Each leaf can be up to six inches (15.2 cm) long. There's only one waxy flower. It may be up to 3.5 inches (8.9 cm) across. When the flower blooms between April and June, it is white. As the flower ages, it turns pink. Never eat the Large-flowered White Trillium's berries or roots—they're poisonous.

LEAVES, PETALS, AND SEPALS IN GROUPS OF THREES

LARGE OVAL LEAVES

WILDFLOWER watcher!

Native Americans used to collect the leaves of the Large-flowered White Trillium for salads or cooked greens. But these plants often die if their leaves are removed.

Laugh Out Loud!

What did the flies say when they landed on the smelly flower?

"This job stinks!"

Foothill Deathcamas

Toxicoscordion paniculatum ORDER **Liliales** ▪ HEIGHT **1–2 ft (0.3–0.6 m)** ▪ HABITAT **Sandy plains and dry, rocky foothill areas** ▪ RANGE **Western United States** ▪ ZONES **3 to 9** ▪ TYPE **Perennial** ▪ Monocot

 This plant's name, Foothill Deathcamas, tells you two things. First, it says where the wildflower grows. You can find it in the foothills of western mountain regions. Second, it tells you that this plant is poisonous. Livestock are the most likely victims. The Foothill Deathcamas is one of the first plants to emerge in the spring. With little else to eat, animals graze on this wildflower. The leaves, stems, and flowers all contain toxins. If an animal eats enough of the plant, it will die. People usually get sick if they eat the poisonous bulbs. The pollen is toxic, too. Only a few species of bees can safely pollinate this wildflower.

→ LOOK FOR THIS
THE FOOTHILL DEATHCAMAS has one straight stem and stands up to two feet (0.6 m) tall. Its five to six thick, grass-like leaves with parallel veins grow from the plant's base. White or cream-colored flowers appear from April to July. Lower flowers grow in bunches. Toward the top, single flowers grow off of the stem. Each flower has six tepals, six stamens, and three styles.

WILDFLOWER watcher!

Wild onions were an important food in Native American diets. Unfortunately, the bulbs of the Foothill Deathcamas look a lot like onions. To avoid making a deadly mistake, Native Americans knew to only dig up the bulbs when both plants had flowers. Then it was easy to tell which plant was which.

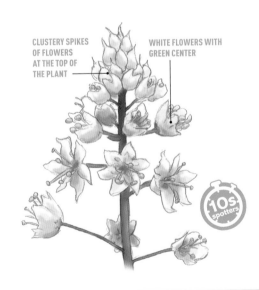

CLUSTERY SPIKES OF FLOWERS AT THE TOP OF THE PLANT

WHITE FLOWERS WITH GREEN CENTER

10s spotters

Corn Lily

Veratrum tenuipetalum ORDER **Liliales** ▪ HEIGHT **4–8 ft (1.2–2.4 m)** ▪ HABITAT **High mountain forests, stream banks, and meadows** ▪ RANGE **Wyoming and Colorado** ▪ ZONES **3 to 8** ▪ TYPE **Perennial** ▪ Monocot

The Corn Lily grows in open, wet places high up in the mountains. It is sometimes found in colonies. This wildflower is a very large plant. It measures up to eight feet (2.4 m) tall when it flowers. Its tall, thick stems point upward. The stems are covered with alternating leaves that have prominent, parallel veins. Like the plant itself, the leaves are large. They can spread up to 12 inches (30.5 cm) wide. Flowers bloom in large clustery spikes at the top of the plant. Each flower has six white petals arranged around a green center. There may be hundreds of flowers on one spike. Flowering is triggered by climate events that are becoming less common, so mass flowering events are also becoming less common. Some years it's difficult to find a flowering plant at all.

WILDFLOWER watcher!

Throughout time, people have found many uses for the Corn Lily. Native Americans used the juice to make poison darts. They made a powder out of the roots to control insects. People also used Corn Lily as a pain reliever. Today, it's used in medicines to slow the heartbeat and lower blood pressure.

CLUSTERY SPIKES OF FLOWERS AT THE TOP OF THE PLANT

WHITE FLOWERS WITH GREEN CENTER

BROAD LEAVES WITH PARALLEL VEINS

10s spotters

DANGER!

The Corn Lily is a very toxic plant. Every part of the plant is poisonous. The roots are especially dangerous. They are five to 10 times more poisonous than the leaves or stems. The toxicity decreases as the plant ages. But the plant is poisonous from the time it starts to grow until it dies.

FLOWER LIFE CYCLE

POPPY FIELD IN BLOOM, CALIFORNIA, U.S.A.

LIKE ALL PLANTS, wildflowers can have one of three different life cycles. Annuals go from seed to flower to seed in one year. Biennials complete their life cycle in two years. And perennials grow for many seasons and may flower for most of them once they are large enough. Regardless of the type of life cycle a wildflower has, all wildflower plants have one goal. They grow so they can reproduce. Flowers, like the ones shown here, are the reproductive parts.

Annuals

Annuals are plants that go from seed to flower to seed in one growing season. When the plant dies, a new generation of plants grows from its seeds the next time environmental events are favorable for growth. For desert annuals, that may take many years. They only germinate when there are unusual amounts of rain. The Desert Poppy (see page 42) is an annual wildflower found in the desert.

DESERT POPPY

COMMON EVENING PRIMROSE

Biennials

Biennials take two years to complete their life cycle. These plants grow leaves and roots the first year. The second year, they produce flowers and seeds. The Common Evening Primrose (see page 63) is a biennial wildflower.

Perennials

Perennials can live for many growing seasons. The top of the plant dies back each year. It regrows the following spring. Most perennials have a specific blooming time. For some plants, blossoms appear for just a few weeks. Other plants produce flowers all summer long. The Goosefoot Violet (see page 59) is a perennial wildflower.

GOOSEFOOT VIOLET

Fairy Slipper

Calypso bulbosa ORDER **Asparagales** ▪ HEIGHT **2– 8 in (5.1–20.3 cm)** ▪ HABITAT **Moist coniferous forests with cool soils** ▪ RANGE **Northern and western United States; throughout Canada, Alaska** ▪ ZONES **4 to 8** ▪ TYPE **Perennial** ▪ Monocot

Many people think the Fairy Slipper is the most beautiful orchid in North America. That's because this plant has a very unusual flower. On top, it has two petals and three sepals. They are purple and magenta. And they sit on top of another unusual petal just like a crown. That third petal has a long scoop-shaped lip. Some people think it looks like a slipper. On the outside, the lip is purple and white with some purple spots. The inside is lined with purple and red veins. And right in the middle there are three rows of white or yellow hairs. The Fairy Slipper has a dainty purple stem. Its one leaf grows down near the ground.

NAME GAME

It's easy to understand how the Fairy Slipper got its common name. People think its modified petal looks like a slipper. To understand how it got its scientific name, you need to know a bit of mythology. Calypso is a sea nymph in Homer's *Odyssey*. Like the character, the Fairy Slipper is beautiful and lives in secluded places.

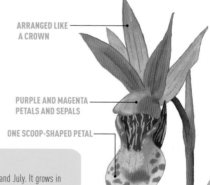

ARRANGED LIKE A CROWN

PURPLE AND MAGENTA PETALS AND SEPALS

ONE SCOOP-SHAPED PETAL

PURPLE STEM

→ LOOK FOR THIS
THE FAIRY SLIPPER blooms between March and July. It grows in partly shady to shady places. Once in a while you might spot a group of these wildflowers growing together. But most of the time these plants are scattered. They usually grow all alone. Fairy Slippers depend on bumblebees for pollination.

Roundleaf Orchid

Galearis rotundifolia ORDER **Asparagales** ◦ HEIGHT **8–14 in (20.3–35.6 cm)** ◦ HABITAT **White-cedar swamps and seepage forests** ◦ RANGE **Northern United States; throughout Canada, Alaska** ◦ ZONES **1 to 7** ◦ TYPE **Perennial** ◦ Monocot

You'd have to be pretty lucky to see a Roundleaf Orchid in the continental United States. They're very rare in the lower 48 states. If you think you found one, take a close look at its flowers. Some people think the Roundleaf Orchid's flowers look like a happy clown. The top part of this wildflower is a pink hood that resembles a clown's head. The bottom is divided into two different parts. First, there are the two white petal-like sepals that stick out to the sides. These are the clown's arms. Then there's the lower lip. It is white with purple spots. If you're imagining a clown, it looks just like the clown's polka-dotted pants.

→ LOOK FOR THIS
THE ROUNDLEAF ORCHID has a single round or oval leaf. That leaf grows right out of the ground. There's only one stem. It grows up from the bottom of the leaf. Between four and 18 irregularly shaped flowers grow from the stem. The flowers bloom in June and July.

FLOWERS: PINK HOOD, WHITE LOWER LIP WITH PURPLE SPOTS

4–18 FLOWERS GROWING FROM THE STEM

ONE STEM

10s spotters

WILDFLOWER watcher!

Worldwide, the Roundleaf Orchid is not a threatened species. But in the United States, it is a rare find. That's because not many places offer a suitable habitat. Only a few northern states have the high-pH, or low-acid, swamps and cedar forests this plant needs to grow. You're more likely to spot it in Canada or Alaska.

GRASS-LIKE LEAVES

Blue-eyed Grass

Sisyrinchium angustifolium ORDER **Asparagales** ◦ HEIGHT **12–18 in (30.5–45.7 cm)** ◦ HABITAT **Meadows; damp fields; low, open woodlands** ◦ RANGE **Eastern United States and southeastern Canada** ◦ ZONES **4 to 9** ◦ TYPE **Perennial** ◦ Monocot

It would be easy to think that the Blue-eyed Grass is a type of grass. Its leaves look just like grass. It grows in clumps like grass does. And the plant's name even has the word "grass" in it. But this plant isn't a grass. It's a wild-flower that blooms between March and June. Its flowers are only about one-half inch (1.3 cm) wide. They have six violet-blue tepals and a yellow center. The flowers grow from branched stems that emerge from the clumps of leaves.

VIOLET-BLUE FLOWER WITH YELLOW CENTER

True **or** False

The Rocky Mountain Iris can bloom in dry meadows.
True. If there was enough snowmelt in the spring, the wildflower can bloom in dry meadows during summer.

All Rocky Mountain Irises are shades of purple.
False. Although rare, the entire flower can be white.

Rocky Mountain Iris

Iris missouriensis ORDER **Asparagales** ◦ HEIGHT **1–2 ft (0.3–0.6 m)** ◦ HABITAT **Marshes, wet meadows, dry steppes, open woodland** ◦ RANGE **Western United States and southwestern Canada** ◦ ZONES **3 to 8** ◦ TYPE **Perennial** ◦ Monocot

THREE VEINED, VIOLET SEPALS WITH YELLOW CENTERS

Flowers of the Rocky Mountain Iris are usually about three inches (7.6 cm) wide. Its three sepals are shades of violet and have a yellow center. That helps

LEAFLESS STALK

THREE PURPLE PETALS

show pollinators where to push the sepals apart to get to the nectar. They often have dark purple veins. The flower's three purple petals are shorter and narrower than the sepals. One or two flowers typically grow from the top of the flower's stout, leafless stalk. Its stiff leaves can grow up to three feet (0.9 m) long.

Laugh Out Loud!

Where did the flowers go on vacation?

Iris I knew!

WHITE FLOWERS WITH SIX TEPALS AND SIX STAMENS ———

YELLOW-ORANGE
ANTHERS ———

Crowpoison

Nothoscordum bivalve ORDER **Asparagales** · HEIGHT **8–16 in (20.3–41.6 cm)** · HABITAT **Lawns, roadsides, prairies, open woodlands** · RANGE **Midwest and southeastern United States** · ZONES **5 to 11** · TYPE **Perennial** · Monocot

Crowpoison is an early spring flower. When it emerges from its bulb, it looks a lot like a wild onion. As it grows, you can see the differences. Crowpoison has fewer flowers than the wild onion. Its flowers are larger. And this wildflower doesn't stink like an onion. Rather, on warm, sunny days, it smells a bit like honey. Crowpoison flowers are white with yellow-orange anthers. They have six tepals and six stamens. The flowers grow in clusters at the top of long, thin stems.

NAME GAME

Crowpoison gets its name from a Cherokee legend. According to the legend, the Cherokee made a poison from this plant. They used the poison to kill the crows that were eating their corn. Some references warn that this plant is poisonous to people. It is unknown if it is also toxic to crows.

UMBEL OF UP TO 40 WHITE, PINK, OR PURPLE FLOWERS

FLOWERS HAVE SIX TEPALS

Tapertip Onion

Allium acuminatum ORDER **Asparagales** · HEIGHT **Up to 12 in (30.5 cm)** · HABITAT **Dry, open, rocky areas** · RANGE **Western United States and southwestern Canada** · ZONES **5 to 9** · TYPE **Perennial** · Monocot

YELLOW ANTHERS

A complex cluster of flowers grows on top of the Tapertip Onion. This cluster is called an umbel. It is a rounded cluster of flowers that radiates out from the tip of the leafless main stem. On the Tapertip Onion, up to 40 flowers may grow on one umbel. These flowers range in color from white to pink to dark purple. Each flower has three inner and three outer tepals. The tepals curve, or taper, out. This characteristic gives the plant its common name. The Tapertip Onion does have a strong onion smell.

Solomon's Plume

Maianthemum racemosum ORDER **Asparagales**
- HEIGHT **1–3 ft (0.3–0.9 m)** · HABITAT **Forests, clearings, and bluffs**
- RANGE **Throughout the United States and Canada** · ZONES **3 to 8**
- TYPE **Perennial** · Monocot

Solomon's Plume has a horizontal stem that branches out underground. Long, arching stems grow up from that underground system in the spring. Each rising stem is covered with large, light-green leaves. These leaves are oval. They have parallel veins and pointed tips. Flowers grow in a branchlike formation at the end of each stem. These flowers are tiny, white, and feathery. They bloom between March and June. When the flowers die off, small green berries appear. As summer approaches, the berries turn ruby red. This wildflower spreads slowly, but it often grows into large colonies in shady areas with rich, loose soil.

DON'T BE FOOLED

Solomon's Plume is similar to another wildflower called Solomon's Seal. To tell the difference, just look at the flowers or berries. In a true Solomon's Seal, the flowers are bell-shaped and yellowish green. They dangle from leaf axils all along the stem. Berries on this wildflower turn bluish black.

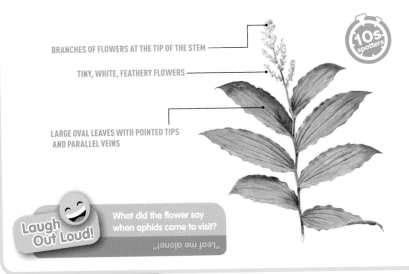

BRANCHES OF FLOWERS AT THE TIP OF THE STEM

TINY, WHITE, FEATHERY FLOWERS

10s spotters

LARGE OVAL LEAVES WITH POINTED TIPS AND PARALLEL VEINS

Laugh Out Loud!

What did the flower say when aphids came to visit?

"Leaf me alone!"

American Lily-of-the-valley

Convallaria majuscula **ORDER Asparagales**
○ **HEIGHT 6–12 in (15.2–30.5 cm)** ○ **HABITAT Open mountain slopes, sandy woodlands, coves** ○ **RANGE Eastern United States** ○ **ZONES 4 to 8**
○ **TYPE Perennial** ○ Monocot

The American Lily-of-the-valley is a small perennial found in a few eastern states. Each plant has two to three leaves and a delicate, drooping flower stalk. The flower stalk is half as long as the leaves. Between 5 and 15 flowers grow from this stalk. These flowers are small, measuring between one-quarter and three-eighths of an inch (0.6– 1 cm) long. But they are beautiful. They look like long white bells with upturned tips and have a wonderfully sweet smell. This wildflower blooms in mid to late spring. It is often found in small colonies, but this plant likes its space. The plants don't grow very close together.

DON'T BE FOOLED

It's not uncommon to see a **Lily-of-the-valley** growing in gardens. Most likely, though, what you're seeing is an introduced species, the European Lily-of-the-valley. The leaves of the native wildflower are longer than those of the European variety. The flower stems are shorter. In addition, the introduced species grows well in colonies of closely spaced plants. The native variety does not.

DELICATE, DROOPING FLOWER STALK

SMALL, WHITE FLOWERS WITH UPTURNED TIPS

DANGER!

Don't even consider eating the American Lily-of-the-valley. Every part of this wildflower is poisonous. The plant produces at least 38 toxins that can affect your heart.

Pickerelweed

Pontederia cordata ORDER **Commelinales** HEIGHT **2–4 ft (0.6–1.2 m)** HABITAT **Marshes and ditches with shallow water** RANGE **Eastern United States, southeastern Canada, Oregon** ZONES **3 to 10** TYPE **Perennial** Monocot

LONG SPIKE PACKED WITH TINY, DEEP BLUE FLOWERS

→ LOOK FOR THIS
THE PICKERELWEED provides a safe habitat for many different organisms. Dragonflies and damselflies lay their eggs on its stem, just above the waterline. Below the waterline, pickerel and other small fish hide among the stems.

The Pickerelweed is an aquatic plant that grows best in full sun. It is found in places that have quiet, shallow water. This wildflower has large heart-shaped leaves. They can be up to five inches (12.7 cm) wide and twice as long. It also has a six-inch (15.2-cm) spike at the end of its stem. This spike is packed with tiny, deep blue flowers. It can take several days for all of the flowers in a spike to bloom. Flowers at the bottom blossom first. Those at the top open up last. Flowers appear from June to October.

SPIKE WITH UP TO 15 LAVENDER FLOWERS

Water Hyacinth

Eichhornia crassipes ORDER **Commelinales** HEIGHT **6–9 in (15.2–22.9 cm)** HABITAT **Lakes, rivers, and ponds in temperate climates** RANGE **Southeastern, southern, and western United States; Hawaii** ZONES **9 to 11** TYPE **Perennial** Monocot

WILDFLOWER watcher!

The Water Hyacinth dies when it freezes. Knowing this, people up north have introduced the Water Hyacinth on purpose. They use it in wastewater treatment areas. The plants clean up the water and absorb some toxic materials.

Invader alert! The Water Hyacinth is native to Brazil. In 1884, it was introduced to the United States at a fair in New Orleans. This floating perennial has a spike of lavender flowers. People saw it as an attractive ornamental plant. But it became a pest. Water Hyacinths can quickly reproduce. Plants grow into a mass of rounded, leathery leaves with dark, feathery dangling roots. The invaders choke waterways and overtake the habitats where they live.

ROUNDED, LEATHERY LEAVES

SPONGY, INFLATED STALKS

Longbract Spiderwort

THREE VIOLET PETALS AND SIX YELLOW-TIPPED STAMENS

THREE HAIRY SEPALS

Tradescantia bracteata ORDER **Commelinales** • HEIGHT **10–16 in (25.4– 40.6 cm)** • HABITAT **Moist prairies, meadows, fields, and roadsides** • RANGE **Northern and midwestern United States** • ZONES **3 to 7** • TYPE **Perennial** • Monocot

The Longbract Spiderwort flowers between May and July. But to see the blossoms on this wildflower, you need to get an early start. These flowers open in the morning and close by midday. And each blossom only lasts for one day. Fortunately, each plant has several flower buds, and only one or two flowers open at a time. The Longbract Spiderwort grows in dense clumps. Each plant has grass-like leaves. Its flowers have three violet petals and six yellow-tipped stamens. The three sepals are hairy, and so are the leaves at the point where they emerge from the stem.

NAME GAME

If you cut the stem of a Longbract Spiderwort, it secretes a sticky substance. As this substance hardens, it becomes threadlike and silky— just like a spiderweb! This trait is how all Spiderworts got their common name.

Prairie Spiderwort

Tradescantia occidentalis ORDER **Commelinales** • HEIGHT **Up to 2 ft (0.6 m)** • HABITAT **Dry, sandy prairies, plains, and meadows; open woodland** • RANGE **Central United States from Texas to northern Plains; south-central Canada** • ZONES **4 to 9** • TYPE **Perennial** • Monocot

THREE EGG-SHAPED PETALS THAT ARE BLUE-VIOLET, WHITE, OR PINK

SIX STAMENS WITH BRIGHT YELLOW TIPS

The flowers of the Prairie Spiderwort grow in clusters at the ends of a branching stem. Each flower measures one to two inches (2.5–5 cm) across. It has three egg-shaped petals, six stamens, and three sepals. The petals may be blue-violet, white, or pink. The sepals are covered in short hairs. This wildflower has long, thin leaves that are smooth but stiff. The Prairie Spiderwort's flowers bloom in the morning and wilt by midday.

→ LOOK FOR THIS

THE SEPALS aren't the only part of a Prairie Spiderwort that are hairy. There are hairs inside the flower, too. Purple filaments hold up the bright yellow stamens. These filaments are lined with purple hairs. To get a good view, it's best to examine them through a magnifier.

Broadleaf Cattail

Typha latifolia ORDER **Poales** ◦ HEIGHT **4–8 ft (1.2–2.4 m)** ◦ HABITAT **Freshwater marshes, swamps, and wetlands** ◦ RANGE **Throughout the United States and Canada** ◦ ZONES **3 to 10** ◦ TYPE **Perennial** ◦ Monocot

When you look at the Broadleaf Cattail, you might not think it has flowers. But it does. In fact, one plant can have more than 1,000 flowers at a time! The flowers are tiny and grow in two parts at the top of a long, stiff stalk. The greenish female flowers grow inside a cylinder at the tip of the stalk. The yellowish male flowers grow on a thin spike that sticks out from the top of the cylinder. The flowers bloom in June and July. After they bloom, the male flowers disappear. Pollinated female flowers grow into a fruit. This fruit looks a bit like a fat brown sausage. Seeds grow inside the fruit.

→ LOOK FOR THIS

IN FALL, the fat brown spike at the top of a Broadleaf Cattail turns yellow. The spike disintegrates in winter. Long slender hairs grow on the seeds. As the cylinder falls apart, the hairs help the seeds blow away in the wind.

FAT BROWN SPIKE AT TOP OF STEM

LONG SWORD-SHAPED LEAVES

CENTRAL STEM UP TO 8 FEET (2.4 M) TALL

Laugh Out Loud! What trees do cattails try to avoid?

Dogwoods.

Broadfruit Bur-reed

Sparganium eurycarpum ORDER **Poales** ▪ HEIGHT **Up to 7 ft (2.1 m)**
▪ HABITAT **Edges of lakes, ponds, and slow-moving streams; channels to swamps and marshes** ▪ RANGE **All but southeastern United States; throughout Canada** ▪ ZONES **3 to 8** ▪ TYPE **Perennial** ▪ **Monocot**

The Broadfruit Bur-reed is a large aquatic plant. It can grow up to seven feet (2.1 m) tall. The central stem of this wildflower branches out. Up to six female flowers and 20 male flowers grow from each branch. The female flowers are up to 1.25 inches (3.2 cm) across. They are shaped like prickly green globes. And while they might look dangerous, they're not. These burrs are even soft to the touch. The male flowers are packed together higher up on each stem. They are smaller than the female flowers. Their color changes from pale yellow to white when they bloom. The Broadfruit Bur-reed blooms for two to three weeks in the summer. Its flowers are pollinated by the wind.

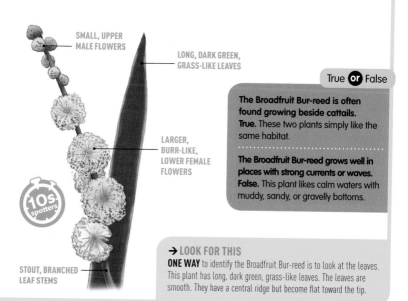

SMALL, UPPER
MALE FLOWERS

LONG, DARK GREEN,
GRASS-LIKE LEAVES

LARGER,
BURR-LIKE,
LOWER FEMALE
FLOWERS

10s
spotters

STOUT, BRANCHED
LEAF STEMS

True **or** False

The Broadfruit Bur-reed is often found growing beside cattails.
True. These two plants simply like the same habitat.

The Broadfruit Bur-reed grows well in places with strong currents or waves.
False. This plant likes calm waters with muddy, sandy, or gravelly bottoms.

→ LOOK FOR THIS
ONE WAY to identify the Broadfruit Bur-reed is to look at the leaves. This plant has long, dark green, grass-like leaves. The leaves are smooth. They have a central ridge but become flat toward the tip.

WILDFLOWER REPORT
TIME TO BLOOM

Autumn Crocus

This wildflower is an Autumn Crocus (see page 24). As you might guess from its name, it blooms in early fall.

WHEN IT COMES TO SEEING WILDFLOWERS, timing is everything. Not all wildflowers are spring bloomers. Some prefer the heat of summer. And others hold on until late fall. Certain flowers bloom for a long time, and others bloom for just one day. Some can even go many years without producing a single flower. The wildflowers on these pages all have blooming patterns that make them unique.

Shoreline Seapurslane

The Shoreline Seapurslane (see page 91) doesn't produce many flowers. But if temperatures are warm enough and water is available, its flowers can bloom all year long.

Monument Plant

The Monument Plant (see page 109) has lots of flowers. When it blooms, each plant can produce up to 600 of them. But you have to be lucky to see them. The Monument Plant can live for up to 80 years, but it flowers only once in its lifetime and then dies.

Nightblooming Cereus

All of the flowers on a Nightblooming Cereus (see page 93) bloom on the same night in June. When the sun rises, the flowers close and die.

THE CAROLINA WILD PETUNIA IS ONE OF THE FIRST WILDFLOWERS IN ITS HABITAT TO BLOOM IN THE SPRING.

California Poppy

Eschscholzia californica ORDER **Ranunculales** • HEIGHT **1–2 ft (0.3–0.6 m)**
• HABITAT **Hillsides, roads, and open areas** • RANGE **Western United States**
• ZONES **6 to 10** • TYPE **Annual/Perennial** • Eudicot

FOUR SILKY, CUP-SHAPED PETALS

WILDFLOWER watcher!

In warmer climates, the California Poppy acts like a perennial. In places with cooler weather, it becomes an annual. This poppy plant cannot survive cold winter temperatures.

The California Poppy grows in large colonies. Each plant has a spreading mat of blue-green, fernlike leaves. Between March and May, bright orange or yellow-orange flowers blossom. With either color, there's a deep orange spot at the flower's base. Only one flower blooms at the end of each long stem. These flowers are one to three inches (2.5–7.6 cm) wide and have four silky petals. They fit together in a cup shape. The flowers open when the sun shines. At night or on rainy or cloudy days, they close. When the flowers die, they are replaced by capsules filled with seeds.

→ **LOOK FOR THIS**
THE DESERT POPPY'S leaves are short and linear. They grow in a mound at the bottom of the plant. The wildflower's bluish green stem has no leaves. The flowers bloom between March and May.

Desert Poppy

Eschscholzia glyptosperma
ORDER **Ranunculales** • HEIGHT **Up to 2–10 in (5.1–25.4 cm)** • HABITAT **Desert washes, flats, and slopes** • RANGE **Southwestern United States** • ZONES **8 to 9** • TYPE **Annual** • Eudicot

ONE FLOWER PER STALK

BLUISH GREEN LEAVES AND STEM

YELLOW-ORANGE FLOWERS WITH FOUR PETALS

The Desert Poppy blooms in spring. It grows at elevations up to 5,000 feet (1,524 m) in the deserts of the southwestern United States. This includes the Mojave and Sonoran Deserts, and parts of the Colorado Desert. Each brightly colored flower has four one-inch (2.5-cm)-long yellow-orange petals. One flower grows on each stalk. The seeds that the Desert Poppy produces float on water. They can easily spread during the rare heavy rains that cause flooding.

Bloodroot

Sanguinaria canadensis
ORDER **Ranunculales** ▪ HEIGHT **6–10 in (15.2–25.4 cm)**
▪ HABITAT **Deciduous forests; upland, floodplain
woodlands** ▪ RANGE **Eastern and central United
States, southeastern Canada** ▪ ZONES **3 to 8**
▪ TYPE **Perennial** ▪ Eudicot

Bloodroot is a type of poppy that blooms in early spring. Flower stalks grow up from underground stems. One leaf and one flower grow from each stalk. The leaf appears first. It is wrapped around the flower bud. As the flower blooms, the leaf uncurls. The flower that appears has eight to ten white petals and yellow stamens in the center. The flower is about 1.5 inches (3.8 cm) in diameter. It opens only in sunlight, and it lives for only one to two days. The round leaves continue to grow even after the flower is gone. They can grow up to nine inches (22.9 cm) across.

NAME GAME

The Bloodroot gets its common name from its underground roots. If you cut them, they release a bright reddish orange sap that looks like blood. Native Americans used this sap as a dye.

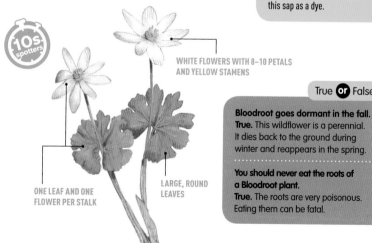

WHITE FLOWERS WITH 8–10 PETALS
AND YELLOW STAMENS

ONE LEAF AND ONE
FLOWER PER STALK

LARGE, ROUND
LEAVES

True **or** False

Bloodroot goes dormant in the fall.
True. This wildflower is a perennial. It dies back to the ground during winter and reappears in the spring.

You should never eat the roots of a Bloodroot plant.
True. The roots are very poisonous. Eating them can be fatal.

Sierra Fumewort

Corydalis caseana ORDER **Ranunculales** HEIGHT **2–3 ft (0.6–0.9 m)** HABITAT **Damp, shady places in mountains** RANGE **Western United States** ZONES **5 to 9** TYPE **Perennial** Eudicot

The Sierra Fumewort is a rare find. You are most likely to see it along mountain streams at mid-level elevations. This is a tall, soft plant. Its hollow stem is covered with large, fernlike leaves. Each year, the plant develops more stems. At the top of each stem is a cluster of long, thin flowers. The flowers are pinkish white and have purple tips. An older plant with lots of stems can have more than 200 flowers in all. The Sierra Fumewort's flowers bloom between June and August. After they bloom, seedpods appear. When the seeds inside the pods are mature, the seedpods explode to disperse the seeds. The same thing happens if you happen to touch one. The seeds also have a little package of food on their sides. This attracts ants that collect the seeds for the food and carry them even farther.

→ LOOK FOR THIS
THE SIERRA FUMEWORT flower has inner and outer petals. The inner petals are closed at the tip. This hides the flower's reproductive parts. But sometimes large pollinators like bumblebees come to visit. When they do, the inner petals open so pollination can take place. Once the bumblebee flies away, the petals close again.

WILDFLOWER watcher!

One of the Sierra Fumewort's most common visitors is the Western Bumblebee. This bee is a nectar robber! Its tongue is too short to reach the nectar. So it bites a hole in the back of the flower and reaches the nectar from there.

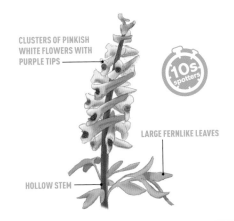

CLUSTERS OF PINKISH WHITE FLOWERS WITH PURPLE TIPS

10s spotters

LARGE FERNLIKE LEAVES

HOLLOW STEM

Dutchman's Breeches

Dicentra cucullaria **ORDER Ranunculales** •
HEIGHT 6–12 in (15.2–30.5 cm) • **HABITAT Rocky woods,
slopes, valleys, and ravines** • **RANGE Eastern United
States, Pacific Northwest, and southeastern Canada** •
ZONES 3 to 7 • **TYPE Perennial** • Eudicot

Dutchman's Breeches grows
best in rocky, shady areas in
deciduous forests. The best places
to look are along gentle slopes,
ravines, and ledges next to streams.
This wildflower earned its common name
from its flowers. The two outer petals are
white, sometimes tipped with pink. The two inner
petals are yellow. Put them together and their
shape resembles an upside-down pair of long,
baggy pants. Several flowers grow in a row up the
plant's stem. The leaves are feathery and grayish
green. But they don't grow on the stem. Instead,
they grow around the plant's base. Dutchman's
Breeches is an early bloomer. Flowers appear
in April and May. After that, the plant goes
dormant and disappears.

WILDFLOWER watcher!

Dutchman's Breeches is common in the eastern United
States. But it appears in the
Pacific Northwest, too.
Scientists have studied the
two populations. They discovered that the species are
nearly identical. And they concluded that the two groups of
flowers were separated about
1,000 years ago.

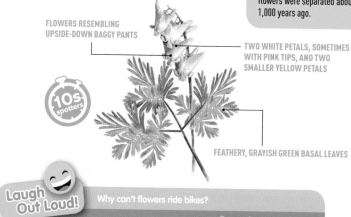

FLOWERS RESEMBLING
UPSIDE-DOWN BAGGY PANTS

TWO WHITE PETALS, SOMETIMES
WITH PINK TIPS, AND TWO
SMALLER YELLOW PETALS

10s spotters

FEATHERY, GRAYISH GREEN BASAL LEAVES

Laugh Out Loud! Why can't flowers ride bikes?

Their petals keep falling off.

PALE GREEN, UMBRELLA-LIKE LEAVES

Mayapple

Podophyllum peltatum ORDER **Ranunculales** ▪ HEIGHT **12–18 in (30.5–45.7 cm)** ▪ HABITAT **Mixed deciduous forests; shady fields, roadsides, and riverbanks** ▪ RANGE **Eastern United States and southeastern Canada** ▪ ZONES **3 to 8** ▪ TYPE **Perennial** ▪ Eudicot

10s. spotters

SINGLE WHITE, WAXY FLOWER

The Mayapple has two leaves and one flower. The two leaves branch out from the plant's stem. They are pale green and shaped like umbrellas. Each one can spread up to a foot (0.3 m) across. The flower grows from the point where the leaves branch off of the stem. It has between six and nine waxy white petals. The flower measures about three inches (7.6 cm) wide. It can be hard to see. It is often hidden under the much larger leaves. Some Mayapples only have one leaf. These Mayapples do not produce a flower.

WILDFLOWER watcher!

Mayapple flowers don't make nectar. For pollination in early spring, they rely on queen bumblebees that are still learning which flowers to visit for nectar. The closer a Mayapple grows to other plants with nectar-bearing flowers, the more often it ends up being pollinated.

WHITE FLOWERS WITH EIGHT PETALS

LEAFLESS STEM

Twinleaf

10s. spotters

Jeffersonia diphylla ORDER **Ranunculales** ▪ HEIGHT **9–18 in (22.9–45.7 cm)** ▪ HABITAT **Limestone soils in rich, damp woods** ▪ RANGE **Eastern United States and southeastern Canada** ▪ ZONES **5 to 7** ▪ TYPE **Perennial** ▪ Eudicot

DON'T BE FOOLED

Twinleaf and Bloodroot bloom at the same time. And their flowers look a lot alike. To tell the difference, look at the leaves. Twinleaf leaves are divided into two equal parts. That's how it got its common name. Bloodroot leaves are round with scalloped edges.

The Twinleaf (*Jeffersonia diphylla*) was named after Thomas Jefferson. In addition to being president, Jefferson loved to grow and study plants. He had many beautiful gardens at Monticello, his home in Virginia. One of the flowers he grew was the Twinleaf. The flowers last for only a few days, but they typically open close to Jefferson's birthday on April 13. Twinleaf grows in a clump. It's only about eight inches (20.3 cm) tall when the white cup-shaped flowers appear. The leafless stalk continues to grow after the flowers die.

BLUE-GREEN LEAVES DIVIDED INTO TWO EQUAL PARTS

Tall Thimbleweed

Anemone virginiana ORDER **Ranunculales** · HEIGHT **2–3 ft (0.6–0.9 m)** ·
HABITAT **Woodlands, forest edges, prairies, meadows, fields**
· RANGE **Central and eastern United States, southern Canada** · ZONES **2 to 8**
· TYPE **Perennial** · Eudicot

To really appreciate the Tall Thimbleweed, you
need to see it at different times of the year. In
the springtime, its greenish white flowers bloom.
The flowers grow on a long stem that rises above
the leaves. Each one has five petal-like sepals and a thimble-
like mound in the middle. That mound is topped with yellow stamens. When
the flowers die, the central mound becomes very noticeable. It turns into a
thimble-shaped seed head. As winter approaches, the thimble turns yellow.
Then it becomes brown. In spring, the seed head opens. It looks like a
fluffy white cotton ball speckled with tiny brown seeds.

THIMBLE-LIKE CENTER WITH
YELLOW STAMENS

WHITE PETAL-LIKE SEPALS

10s spotters

Make your own neighborhood
wildflower field guide.

1. Grab a cell phone to take photos.
   You'll also need a notebook, a pen,
   and a tape measure.
2. Search for different types of wildflowers
   in your area. Take photos of flowers in
   bloom and record the dates.
3. Measure and record details about each
   plant. Make sketches.
4. Summarize your notes. Then conduct
   research to learn the scientific and
   common names of each species
   you found.
5. Download your photos to a computer
   and combine them with your notes
   and sketches. Add new wildflowers
   as you find them.

Laugh Out Loud!

Why did the little flower jump
around the room?

It was a wildflower.

Hairy Clematis

Clematis hirsutissima ORDER **Ranunculales** · HEIGHT **2 ft (0.6 m)** · HABITAT **Grasslands, sagebrush plains, and ponderosa pine forests** · RANGE **Western United States** · ZONES **6 to 9** · TYPE **Perennial** · Eudicot

Meet the Hairy Clematis, a wildflower so hairy that its seeds can be used to insulate shoes! Most members of the *Clematis* genus are vines. The Hairy Clematis is not. It is a two-foot (0.6-m)-tall plant with a straight stalk and a single large flower on the top. The stalk curves down toward the ground at the top. Several stems with spear-shaped leaves grow off the stalk. The bell-shaped flower of the Hairy Clematis doesn't have any petals. Instead it has four leathery sepals. On the outside, the sepals are covered with glistening, silvery hairs. On the inside, they are dark purple. Their pointed tips flare out to reveal lots of hairy, white stamens and filaments inside.

NAME GAME

The Hairy Clematis has several different common names. One name is the Vase Flower, which refers to the flower's shape. It got the name Lion's Beard because of its shaggy fruit head. Even the wildflower's scientific name says something about its appearance. The Latin word *hirsutissima* means "very hairy." Both the flowers and stalk are hairy.

→ LOOK FOR THIS
THE HAIRY CLEMATIS blooms between April and July. After that, the fruit head develops. It is covered by long, soft, feathery hairs. By at least one account, the shaggy fruit head gives the flower a "Dr. Seuss look."

10s spotters

SILVERY HAIRS ON OUTSIDE OF SEPALS

HAIRY, WHITE STAMENS AND FILAMENTS

DARK PURPLE COLOR ON INSIDE OF SEPALS

BELL-SHAPED FLOWER THAT FLARES OUT AT THE TIPS

Dwarf Larkspur

VIOLET, BLUE, OR WHITE FLOWERS

Delphinium tricorne ORDER **Ranunculales** ▫ HEIGHT **12–30 in (30.5–76.2 cm)**
▫ **HABITAT Moist woodlands** ▫ RANGE **Mid-Atlantic, midwestern, and southeastern
United States** ▫ ZONES **4 to 8** ▫ TYPE **Perennial** ▫ Eudicot

Each flower on a Dwarf Larkspur has five petal-like
sepals and four petals. The sepals are typically
violet but can also be white or blue. The two upper
petals are short and white. The two lower petals
are larger, hairy, and the same color as the sepals.
At the top of the flower, the upper sepal stretches
out to form a spur. This spur contains a pair of
nectar chambers. It attracts bees, butterflies,
and the Ruby-throated Hummingbird. Leaves grow
toward the bottom of the stem. They are divided
into thin, spear-shaped sections.

FIVE PETAL-LIKE SEPALS
AND FOUR PETALS

NAME GAME

The Dwarf Larkspur belongs to
the *Delphinium* genus. The
Greek word *delphinium* means
"dolphin." Some people think
Delphinium seedpods are
shaped like dolphins.

SINGLE STEM WITH REDDISH BASE   DEEP PURPLISH BLUE FLOWERS

Twolobe Larkspur

Delphinium nuttallianum ORDER **Ranunculales** ▫ HEIGHT **6–30 in (15.2–76.2 cm)**
▫ **HABITAT Dry foothills, valleys, and sagebrush deserts** ▫ RANGE **Western United States and
southwestern Canada** ▫ ZONES **4 to 8** ▫ TYPE **Perennial** ▫ Eudicot

FLOWERS HAVE FIVE
SEPALS AND FOUR PETALS.

The Twolobe Larkspur grows in dry, open areas of the
western United States. It has a single stem with a
reddish base. Each plant has between two and six
leaves. The leaves are divided into rounded, spear-
shaped lobes. They grow from the bottom quarter
of the plant's stem. Deep purplish blue flowers bloom from March to July.
One plant may have up to 15 flowers. The flowers grow on short
stems that branch off of the main stem.
Their five sepals spread out wide to reveal
the four shorter petals inside. Because
the top sepal angles back over the nectar
chambers, these flowers are twice as long
as they are wide.

DANGER!

Plants that belong to the
Delphinium genus should
never be eaten. All parts of
these plants are toxic.

Red Columbine

Aquilegia canadensis ORDER **Ranunculales**
- HEIGHT **2–3 ft (0.6–0.9 m)** - HABITAT **Woodland edges, riverbanks, gravelly shores and ridges** - RANGE **Eastern half of United States, southeastern Canada**
- ZONES **3 to 8** - TYPE **Perennial** - Eudicot

The Red Columbine is well known for its flashy flowers. These drooping, bell-like blooms can be up to two inches (5 cm) long. They are bright red and yellow. Bright red spurs—which some people think look like eagle talons—stick out on top. And lots of bushy yellow stamens peek out below the petals. The plant's leaves are attractive, too. Each one is divided into three rounded lobes. When the Red Columbine's flowers bloom in late spring, they attract hummingbirds and butterflies. To find a Red Columbine, be sure to look in the shade. Continuous sunlight can burn the Red Columbine's leaves and stunt the plant's growth.

True or False

Native Americans have used the Red Columbine to make a love charm.
True. Men rubbed crushed seeds on their hands. They believed this would attract a love interest's attention.

The Red Columbine smells as good as it looks.
False. This beautiful flower has no scent. Luckily, the hummingbirds that pollinate it are attracted to colors and not smells. Hummingbirds can't smell.

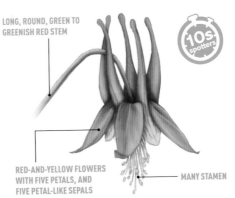

LONG, ROUND, GREEN TO GREENISH RED STEM

10s. spotters

RED-AND-YELLOW FLOWERS WITH FIVE PETALS, AND FIVE PETAL-LIKE SEPALS

MANY STAMEN

Laugh Out Loud! Why is Red Columbine such a flashy flower?

It has great style.

Early Saxifrage

Saxifraga virginiensis ORDER **Saxifragales** ▪ HEIGHT **Up to 15 in (38.1 cm)** ▪ HABITAT **Dry rocky slopes and outcrops** ▪ RANGE **Eastern United States and Canada** ▪ ZONES **5 to 9** ▪ TYPE **Perennial** ▪ Eudicot

During winter, the Early Saxifrage is just a ring of leaves growing on the ground. These leaves are oval and have hairy, scalloped edges. And they might be bright red. But come spring, the leaves turn green. Then the hairy stem begins to grow. Branches of flower buds start to appear. Clusters of tiny white flowers bloom on each branch. They are just a quarter inch (0.6 cm) across. Each flower has five white oblong petals and ten yellow stamens. Up to 30 of these tiny flowers can grow on one plant. The Early Saxifrage blooms between February and June.

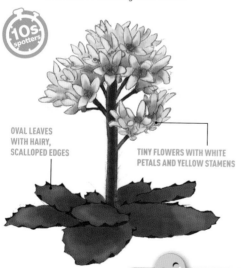

10s spotters

OVAL LEAVES WITH HAIRY, SCALLOPED EDGES

TINY FLOWERS WITH WHITE PETALS AND YELLOW STAMENS

NAME GAME

The name "saxifrage" comes from two Latin words. *Saxum* means "rock." And *frangere* means "to break." This wildflower is often found growing between the cracks in rocks. Often it looks like the plant caused a crack to appear.

Laugh Out Loud!

What do you call a garden filled with lots of different wildflowers?

A polli-nation.

NECTAR SPUR ON TOP OF FLOWER

Smallflower Woodland-star

Lithophragma parviflorum ORDER **Saxifragales**
• HEIGHT **4–12 in (10.2–30.5 cm)** • HABITAT **Prairies, among sagebrush, and forest openings at lower elevations** • RANGE **Western United States and southwestern Canada** • ZONES **5 to 8** • TYPE **Perennial** • Eudicot

FIVE PETAL-LIKE SEPALS AND FOUR PETALS

PINK OR WHITE FLOWERS

Each flower on the Smallflower Woodland-star has five petals. Each petal is divided into three parts. Put all the petals together, and the flower earns its common name. It really does look like a star. That star emerges from a bud at the top of a slender, hairy, purple stem. But it doesn't blossom all alone. Each plant can produce up to 11 white or pink flowers. This wildflower's leaves grow at the base of the stem. Like the petals, they are divided into smaller parts.

Laugh Out Loud!

Why were all the wildflowers afraid of the baker?

So many recipes called for a cup of flour.

Heartleaf Foamflower

Tiarella cordifolia ORDER **Saxifragales** • HEIGHT **9–12 in (22.9–30.5 cm)**
• HABITAT **Cool, moist, deciduous forests; stream banks** • RANGE **Eastern United States and southeastern Canada** • ZONES **4 to 9** • TYPE **Perennial** • Eudicot

LONG STAMENS

SPIKES OF TINY, WHITE, STAR-SHAPED FLOWERS

The Heartleaf Foamflower has spikes of flowers. These spikes rise above a mound of heart-shaped leaves. The flowers are tiny, white, and shaped like stars. The stamens in these flowers are very long. This makes the plant look foamy or frothy, which is how this wildflower got its common name. The Heartleaf Foamflower blooms from April to July. It grows in shady, woody places. The wildflower reproduces with horizontal stems called runners.

WILDFLOWER watcher!

The Heartleaf Foamflower grows from Georgia to Nova Scotia. All plants have heart-shaped leaves at their base. But southern plants also have small leaves growing on their stalks. Northern plants don't.

Mountain Wood Sorrel

Oxalis montana ORDER **Oxalidales** · HEIGHT **Less than 4 in (10.2 cm)** · HABITAT **Rich, damp woodlands** · RANGE **Eastern United States and southeastern Canada** · ZONES **3 to 9** · TYPE **Perennial** · Eudicot

The Mountain Wood Sorrel is a graceful little wildflower. Its leaves are each divided into three smaller heart-shaped leaflets. Its flowers grow on short stalks. There is only one flower per stalk. But one plant can have up to 34 stalks. Each flower has five petals. The petals are white with pink veins. Each petal has a yellow dot at the bottom. As the veins bleed together, they create a circle around these dots. The Mountain Wood Sorrel is found in cool, moist woods. It blooms between May and July.

FIVE PETALS

WHITE FLOWERS WITH PINK VEINS

WILDFLOWER watcher!

The leaves of the Mountain Wood Sorrel don't grow on stems. They grow directly from the roots.

Slender Yellow Wood Sorrel

Oxalis dillenii ORDER **Oxalidales** · HEIGHT **Up to 15 in (38.1 cm)** · HABITAT **Fields, glades, lawns, prairies, and roadsides** · RANGE **Most of the United States and southern Canada** · ZONES **8 to 11** · TYPE **Perennial** · Eudicot

LIGHT GREEN LEAVES DIVIDED INTO THREE HEART-SHAPED PARTS

YELLOW FLOWERS

THIN, HAIRY STEMS

The Slender Yellow Wood Sorrel is a native wildflower. But to many people, it's just a weed. This plant has a deep taproot. Underground, smaller, stringy roots grow out from that main root. Aboveground, multiple thin, hairy stems grow up from the base. Each stem produces clusters of leaves. And each leaf is divided into three little leaflets that are shaped like hearts. The Slender Yellow Wood Sorrel's yellow flowers bloom between May and November. Each one has five sepals, five petals, 10 stamens, and one pistil.

True **or** False

Wood Sorrels are shamrocks.
False. Because of the shape of their leaves, many people think these plants are shamrocks. But they're not. The term "shamrock" refers to clovers.

Wood Sorrels are edible.
True. The leaves, flowers, and immature green seed-pods are all edible. But they are a bit sour.

ATTRACTING POLLINATORS

Scarlet Monkeyflower

Hummingbirds are attracted to the Scarlet Monkeyflower's (see page 124) big reddish orange flowers. They pollinate flowers when they go after the nectar in the flower's long tubes.

SOME WILDFLOWERS ARE POLLINATED BY WIND.

Others pollinate themselves. But more than 80 percent of flowering plants depend on pollinators to help them out. A pollinator is an organism that transfers pollen from the male anther of a flower to the female stigma. Common pollinators include ants, bats, bees, birds, butterflies, flies, and wasps. Unusual ones include lizards, mosquitoes, and small mammals. The color, size, shape, and smell of flowers like the ones shown here determine which pollinators will visit.

Rocky Mountain Iris

Flowers on a Rocky Mountain Iris (see page 32) have a yellow center. This spot tells pollinators where to push the sepals apart so they can get to the nectar. Many flowers have "nectar guides" on their petals to help pollinators find the nectar reward. Some of these cues are only visible to animals that can see ultraviolet light, which people can't see without the help of special equipment.

Red Trillium

Red Trillium (see page 25) uses smell to attract its pollinators. But that smell isn't pleasant. This flower reeks like a wet dog. It attracts flies that lay their eggs in the rotting flesh of dead animals.

A BEE VISITS A CALIFORNIA POPPY.

Common St. John's Wort

Hypericum perforatum **ORDER Malpighiales**
▫ **HEIGHT 1–3 ft (0.3–0.9 m)** ▫ **HABITAT Grasslands, pastures, meadows, rangelands, and forest clearings** ▫ **RANGE Most of the United States and southern Canada** ▫ **ZONES 3 to 8** ▫ **TYPE Perennial** ▫ Eudicot

 Common St. John's Wort is a tall, thin perennial—and an invader. It is native to Europe, North Africa, and parts of Asia. In 1696, a religious group brought the plant to Pennsylvania in the U.S. Now, more than 300 years later, this wildflower has spread across the country. It is classified as a noxious weed in eight western states. Common St. John's Wort grows in dense patches and is mixed in with other plants. Just one plant can have up to 30 reddish, woody stems. Flowers grow in clusters at the end of each stem. The flowers have five petals. They have yellow or bright yellow-orange petals with little black dots. The plant's leaves are covered with small, clear dots. The substances in these dots are poisonous.

WILDFLOWER watcher!

Common St. John's Wort is very successful at reproduction. One plant can produce up to 23,000 seeds in its lifetime. These seeds can remain underground for up to 10 years before they grow into a plant. New plants can also sprout from underground root buds.

Common St. John's Wort has been used to treat everything from depression to skin disorders. Throughout history, people have also believed it had magical powers. Some people thought the plants could protect them from witches and evil spirits. Others carried bits of the plant around as good luck charms.

YELLOW OR BRIGHT YELLOW-ORANGE FLOWER WITH FIVE PETALS

MANY WOODY STEMS, UP TO 3 FEET (0.9 M) TALL

LEAVES COVERED WITH SMALL, CLEAR DOTS

10s spotters

Tinker's Penny

Hypericum anagalloides ORDER **Malpighiales**
HEIGHT **1–3 in (2.5–7.6 cm)** HABITAT **Bogs, marshes, and wetlands** RANGE **Western United States and southwestern Canada** ZONES **5 to 9** TYPE **Annual/Perennial** Eudicot

Tinker's Penny is a small wildflower common across western North America. This plant grows only up to three inches (7.6 cm) high. But it has runners, or horizontal stems. Because of this, Tinker's Penny can spread into a thick mat that covers the ground. Most of this mat consists of tiny green, egg-shaped leaves. Pairs of leaves grow opposite each other up each stem. Each plant can also produce up to 15 flowers. The flowers have five sepals, five petals, and up to 25 stamens. They are yellow or salmon-yellow in color and grow at the top of short stalks. The flowers bloom from May to September.

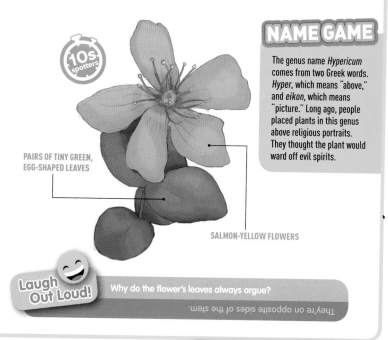

10s spotters

PAIRS OF TINY GREEN, EGG-SHAPED LEAVES

SALMON-YELLOW FLOWERS

NAME GAME

The genus name *Hypericum* comes from two Greek words. *Hyper*, which means "above," and *eikon*, which means "picture." Long ago, people placed plants in this genus above religious portraits. They thought the plant would ward off evil spirits.

Laugh Out Loud! Why do the flower's leaves always argue?

They're on opposite sides of the stem.

BLUE-VIOLET FLOWERS WITH WHITE THROATS

Common Blue Violet

Viola sororia ORDER **Malpighiales** · HEIGHT **6–10 in (15.2 –25.4 cm)**
· HABITAT **Open woodlands, black soil prairies, savannas, and wooded slopes
along rivers or lakes** · RANGE **Eastern and central United States; southeastern
and central Canada** · ZONES **3 to 7** · TYPE **Annual/Perennial** · Eudicot

The Common Blue Violet is so pretty that four
states chose it to be their state flower (see pages
138–139). This low-growing perennial blooms from
April to August. It has large blue-violet flowers
with white throats. Occasionally, the petals are
white and have purple veins. The stalks that these
flowers droop from are leafless. They rise above a
mass of glossy, wide, heart-shaped leaves. These
violets are often seen in woods and prairies. They
often grow in lawns, where some people love the
pretty flowers, and others consider them weeds.

WILDFLOWER watcher!

Some violets have exploding
fruits. The seeds that shoot out
have little food packets on
them. This attracts ants, which
carry the seeds away. After the
ants eat the food packets, they
discard the rest of the seed in
their waste dumps. This is how
the ants plant the seeds.

**→ LOOK FOR THIS
THE FIELD PANSY'S** petals are
bilaterally symmetrical. That means
if you cut the flower down the
middle, the left side would be the
mirror image of the right.

PALE VIOLET-BLUE PETALS,
WHITE AT BASE

Field Pansy

Viola bicolor ORDER **Malpighiales**
· HEIGHT **6 in (15.2 cm)** · HABITAT
**Pastures, roadsides, lawns, and other
disturbed areas** · RANGE **Most of the
United States and Canada** · ZONES
4 to 9 · TYPE **Annual** · Eudicot

Thanks to its weedy nature, the Field Pansy
has made its way across North America.
This native wildflower grows well in full or
partial sun. Its long, slender leaves alternate
up a green or purple stem. This wildflower
has five sepals and five petals. The petals
are a pale blue-violet with dark purple veins.
The base of the flower's petals is mostly
white, with a yellow patch at the bottom of
the lowest petal. And the two side petals are
covered with white hairs.

LOWEST PETAL
HAS YELLOW
SPOT AT BASE. TWO SIDE
PETALS ARE
BEARDED
AT BASE.

Goosefoot Violet

Viola purpurea ORDER **Malpighiales**
• HEIGHT **2–6 in (5.1–15.2 cm)** • HABITAT **Open, rocky, fairly dry slopes at moderate to high mountain elevations** • RANGE **Western United States; southwestern Canada and central Canada** • ZONES **3 to 8** • TYPE **Perennial** • Eudicot

Not all violets are purple or blue as their name suggests. The Goosefoot Violet's flowers are lemon yellow. Each flower has five petals. The lower three petals usually have thin, brown lines on them. These lines, which look a little like pencil markings, reach deep into the flower's throat. A hairy, yellow beard grows at the base of the two side petals. The backside of these petals is brownish purple. The plant's flowers hang from the tips of thin stalks. These stalks rise over a bed of thick, fleshy leaves. The leaves are purplish green and have noticeable veins. They are wedge-shaped and their edges are ridged.

True **or** False

The Goosefoot Violet is the only yellow violet.
False. There are many other yellow violet species. And some violets are white.

The Goosefoot Violet is an endangered species.
False. This wildflower is common throughout the western United States. There are eight subspecies.

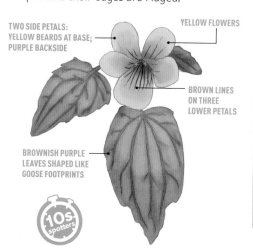

TWO SIDE PETALS: YELLOW BEARDS AT BASE; PURPLE BACKSIDE

YELLOW FLOWERS

BROWN LINES ON THREE LOWER PETALS

BROWNISH PURPLE LEAVES SHAPED LIKE GOOSE FOOTPRINTS

10s spotters

NAME GAME

The Goosefoot Violet's common name makes a lot of sense. Some people think its leaves are shaped like a goose footprint. The wildflower's scientific name is a different story. The Latin word *purpurea* means "purple." Lots of violets are purple. But this one's flowers are usually yellow.

PALE BLUE FLOWERS

SMALL, NARROW GREEN LEAVES

10s spotters

Prairie Flax

Linum lewisii ORDER **Malpighiales** • HEIGHT **18–20 in (45.7–50.8 cm)**
• HABITAT **Woodlands, prairies, meadows, and fields** • RANGE **Central and western United States, Alaska, throughout Canada** • ZONES **3 to 9**
• TYPE **Perennial** • Eudicot

→ LOOK FOR THIS
PRAIRIE FLAX stems are straight. But they don't usually stand up straight. If you see this plant, the stems are more than likely leaning toward the ground. That's how this wildflower grows.

Prairie Flax is a native, semi-evergreen, perennial wildflower. Little green leaves alternate their way up its woody stems. As the plant ages, the leaves fall off. Each plant produces multiple flowers. The flowers measure about 1.5 inches (3.8 cm) across. Those at the bottom of a stem bloom first. This wildflower's most common pollinators are flies and bees. But in order to succeed, they must work very quickly. Prairie Flax has a one-day flowering period. Blossoms open up in the morning. By afternoon, the petals fall off.

Berlandier's Yellow Flax

Linum berlandieri ORDER **Malpighiales** • HEIGHT **6 in (15.2 cm)**
• HABITAT **Dry, rocky, sandy prairies** • RANGE **South-central United States**
• ZONES **6 to 9** • TYPE **Annual/Perennial** • Eudicot

ORANGISH YELLOW FLOWERS WITH COPPER-COLORED VEINS

RIGID, GREEN STEMS

10s spotters

GRAYISH GREEN, POINTED LEAVES

Berlandier's Yellow Flax has rigid, green stems. Its grayish green leaves are stiff and pointed. These parts are as rugged as the ground where the wildflower grows. Its flowers are a different story. The petals are barely attached to the plant. If you touch them, even slightly, they'll fall off. And if you don't touch them, the petals will only remain attached for one or two days. As this wildflower's name suggests, Berlandier's Yellow Flax has orangish yellow petals. The petals are oval and have notched edges. Each one is lined with copper-colored veins.

→ LOOK FOR THIS
BERLANDIER'S YELLOW FLAX flowers measure between one and two inches (2.5–5 cm) wide. Parts in these flowers come in fives. There are five petals, five sepals, five stamens, and five styles. Even the plant's fruit, which develops in pollinated flowers, has five segments. Two small, flat, brown seeds grow in each segment.

Spotted Geranium

Geranium maculatum **ORDER Geraniales** ∘ **HEIGHT 1–2.5 ft (0.3–0.8 m)** ∘ **HABITAT Woods, thickets, and shaded roadsides** ∘ **RANGE Eastern half of United States, southeastern Canada** ∘ **ZONES 3 to 8** ∘ **TYPE Perennial** ∘ **Eudicot**

The flowers of the Spotted Geranium are lilac or pink. Their five petals face upward and fit together in the shape of a saucer. These blooms first appear in March or April. But there's no rush to see them because the plant produces flowers for up to seven weeks. The Spotted Geranium's dark green leaves are just as showy as its flowers. They grow in a mound that may be up to two feet (0.6 m) high and 18 inches (45.7 cm) across. Each leaf is about six inches (15.2 cm) across and is divided into five deeply cut parts.

LILAC OR PINK, FIVE-PETALED FLOWERS

DARK GREEN LEAVES WITH FIVE DEEPLY CUT LOBES

→ LOOK FOR THIS
THREE TO FOUR WEEKS after the Spotted Geranium's flowers die back, its fruit appears. This fruit is shaped like the head and beak of a crane.

Redstem Stork's Bill

SMALL, PINK, FIVE-PETALED FLOWERS

Erodium cicutarium **ORDER Geraniales** ∘ **HEIGHT Up to 2 ft (0.6 m)** ∘ **HABITAT Grassy open places, disturbed areas, roadsides** ∘ **RANGE Throughout most of the United States and Canada** ∘ **ZONES 8 to 10** ∘ **TYPE Annual/Biennial** ∘ **Eudicot**

Redstem Stork's Bill is a Eurasian plant that has spread throughout the world. In the U.S., it grows in every state except Florida. This wildflower produces small, five-petaled, pink blossoms. The flowers grow in clusters with two to 10 flowers each. They bloom at the tip of hairy red stems. Fernlike leaves grow at the bottom of the plant. They can be up to eight inches (20.3 cm) long and 2.5 inches (6.4 cm) wide. A few smaller leaflets may grow up the stem.

HAIRY RED STEM

WILDFLOWER watcher!

The Redstem Stork's Bill's seeds can bury themselves! As the wildflower's fruit dries up, it flings the seeds away from the mother plant. The seeds unwind when they're wet. They rewind when they dry out. Over time, the seeds drill their way into the ground.

Sticky Purple Geranium

Geranium viscosissimum ORDER Geraniales · HEIGHT Up to 16–36 in (40.6–91.4 cm) · HABITAT Foothills, canyons, open woodlands, and mountain meadows · RANGE Western United States and southwestern Canada · ZONES 2 to 8 · TYPE Annual/Perennial · Eudicot

The Sticky Purple Geranium lives up to its name. The flowers on this geranium have five sepals and five petals. The petals, which are hairy on the lower half, range in color from lavender to deep purple. They also have purple veins. The wildflower's palm-shaped leaves are mainly found at the plant's base. Both the leaves and the plant's long stem are covered with flat, stiff hairs. These hairs produce a sticky substance. This substance helps the plant get food. When insects land on the leaves, they get stuck. As the leaf dissolves the insect, the plant absorbs the nutrients. This trait helps the plant survive in nutrient-poor environments.

DON'T BE FOOLED

The Sticky Purple Geranium is easily confused with Richardson's Geranium. But there are major differences. The Sticky Purple Geranium has darker-colored petals. Richardson's Geranium petals are pale pink or white. And the Sticky Purple Geranium's leaves and stem are covered with hairs. Richardson's Geranium only has hairs along the veins on the lower sides of its leaves.

LAVENDER TO DEEP PURPLE FLOWERS WITH PURPLE VEINS

10s spotters

STEMS COVERED WITH HAIRS

SOFT HAIRS ON LOWER HALF OF FLOWERS

Laugh Out Loud! Why did the Sticky Purple Geranium stay home from school?

It was feeling blue.

Pinkladies

SLENDER, DOWNY CENTRAL STEM THAT BRANCHES AT THE TOP

ROSY PINK, WRINKLY, POPPY-LIKE FLOWERS

Oenothera speciosa ORDER **Myrtales** • HEIGHT **Up to 2 ft (0.6 m)** • HABITAT **Grasslands, meadows, woodland edges, and forest clearings** • RANGE **Southern half of United States** • ZONES **4 to 9** • TYPE **Perennial** • Eudicot

Pinkladies have long spindly buds. When the buds open, they reveal fragrant, poppy-like flowers. Each blossom has four rosy pink petals with darker pink veins. The wrinkly petals fade to white at their base. But the throat of the flower is bright yellow. Its eight stamens have white or yellow anthers. And the white stigma in the middle is shaped like a cross at its tip. These wildflowers tend to sprawl as they grow. They can expand to form very large colonies of wildflowers.

SPEAR-SHAPED LEAVES WITH UNEVEN EDGES

→ LOOK FOR THIS
PINKLADIES growing in the southern part of this wildflower's range open just before dawn. They stay open until the sun shines directly on them.

Common Evening Primrose

10 S. spotters

Oenothera biennis ORDER **Myrtales** • HEIGHT **3–6 ft (0.9–1.8 m)** • HABITAT **Dry, open fields; along roadsides; disturbed areas; open woodlands** • RANGE **Most of the United States and southern Canada** • ZONES **4 to 9** • TYPE **Biennial** • Eudicot

FOUR YELLOW PETALS

PROMINENT STAMENS

The Common Evening Primrose lives for two years. The first year, it produces a stubby cluster of light green, spear-shaped leaves. The second year, it takes off. A tall central stem grows up to six feet (1.8 m) high. The green stem has a purple tinge, and it is covered with white hairs. The stem may have one or two main branches. And it has so many leaves that it looks bushy. A cluster of yellow flowers grows at the top of each main stem. The flowers have four petals and prominent stamens. And they smell like lemons!

WILDFLOWER watcher!

Native Americans found many uses for the Common Evening Primrose. They ate the roots, shoots, and leaves. They made bandages out of different plant parts to treat boils and bruises. And they chewed the roots to increase their strength. They even made tea to treat laziness and "overfatness."

Pinkfairies

Clarkia pulchella **ORDER Myrtales** • **HEIGHT 6–18 in (15.2–45.7 cm)** • **HABITAT Dry, open slopes at low to mid elevations** • **RANGE Northwestern United States; British Columbia, Canada** • **ZONES 3 to 8** • **TYPE Annual** • Eudicot

Pinkfairies are easy to identify. Each flower has four dark pink petals. Each petal is divided into three lobes. The middle lobe is twice as wide as the other two. And the base of each petal is long and narrow. The flower has four sepals, four stigmas, and eight stamens. Only the outer four stamens produce pollen. Its one pistil looks like a tiny white flower growing in the middle of the bloom. These wildflowers can grow up to 18 inches (45.7 cm) tall. Their freely branching stems are covered with fine, flat hairs. Their leaves look like blades of grass. The flowers bloom in early summer.

NAME GAME

In 1806, Meriwether Lewis discovered a delicate flower while exploring Idaho. He collected a specimen. His partner, William Clark, described the flower in great detail but didn't give it a name. Eight years later, botanist Frederick Pursh named the species *Clarkia pulchella*. In Latin, *pulchella* means "beautiful." Now, that wildflower that had no name also has several common names. It is known as Pinkfairies, Ragged Robin, Deerhorn Clarkia, and Beautiful Clarkia.

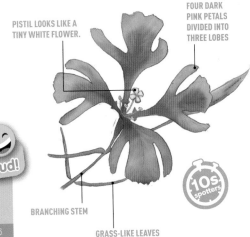

PISTIL LOOKS LIKE A TINY WHITE FLOWER.

FOUR DARK PINK PETALS DIVIDED INTO THREE LOBES

BRANCHING STEM

GRASS-LIKE LEAVES

Laugh Out Loud!

Knock knock.
Who's there?
Annual.
Annual who?
Ann-u-al thought this joke was going to be funny!

10s spotters

Fireweed

Chamerion angustifolium ORDER **Myrtales**
• HEIGHT **2–6 ft (0.6–1.8 m)** • HABITAT **Open
meadows; along streams, roadsides, and forest
edges** • RANGE **All but southeastern United States;
throughout Canada, Alaska** • ZONES **2 to 7** • TYPE
Perennial • Eudicot

If an area is burned by fire,
Fireweed is one of the first
plants to reappear. It is a tall,
hardy perennial that grows well
in many environments. Sometimes
very large numbers of the plant grow
in clusters, covering a large area. This wild-
flower has a long stem. It typically grows up to six feet (1.8 m). But sometimes it soars up to nine feet (2.7 m) tall! The stem is crowded with long,
narrow leaves. A spike of flowers grows at the top. One spike can have up
to 50 rosy purple blooms. The flowers first open from the bottom of the
spike. As the flowers wither, they are replaced by long, narrow seedpods.
Each tiny seed in the pod has a tuft of silky hairs. These hairs act like
parachutes. They help the seeds travel in the wind.

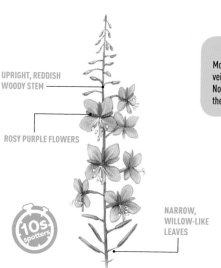

UPRIGHT, REDDISH
WOODY STEM

ROSY PURPLE FLOWERS

NARROW,
WILLOW-LIKE
LEAVES

**10s
spotters**

WILDFLOWER watcher!

Most plants have straight or branching
veins. Their veins extend to the leaf edge.
Not Fireweed! Its veins are circular. And
they don't touch the edge of the leaf.

→ LOOK FOR THIS
FIREWEED flowers have four
petals and four sepals. The petals
are broad and round at the tip
and taper in at their base. Along
with the narrow sepals, they give
the flower a saucerlike shape.
Up to eight long, white stigmas
stick out from the middle of
each bloom.

Winged Lythrum

Lythrum alatum ORDER **Myrtales** · HEIGHT **1–4 ft (0.3–1.2 m)**
- HABITAT **Moist fields, meadows, ditches, and roadsides; pond and stream edges**
- RANGE **Eastern two-thirds of United States; Ontario, Canada**
- ZONES **3 to 8** · TYPE **Perennial** · Eudicot

The sepals of a Winged Lythrum fit together to form a winged floral tube. A flower grows at the edge of each tube. These flowers are small, measuring between a quarter and a half inch (0.6–1.3 cm) across. Each flower has six petals. The petals look and feel like wrinkled tissue paper. They are pale lavender or rosy pink and have a dark purple vein running down the middle. These lines lead straight into the deep, white throat of the flower. Spear-shaped leaves alternate their way up the plant's four-sided stem. As the stem rises, the leaves get smaller. Winged Lythrum flowers bloom in mid to late summer. The plants can flower for up to two months.

DON'T BE FOOLED

Some people confuse Winged Lythrum with its Eurasian cousin, Purple Loosestrife. Purple Loosestrife is larger and has wingless stems. Its slender, willow-like leaves are hairy. Purple Loosestrife is a noxious weed. Winged Lythrum is not.

True or False

Winged Lythrum is native to the U.S. True.

The Winged Lythrum is one of the dominant plants where it grows. False. Many wetland grasses are taller. Because of this, the Winged Lythrum often has trouble competing for space.

SPEAR-SHAPED LEAVES

10s. spotters

FLOWERS: SIX PETALS;
PALE LAVENDER OR ROSY PINK;
DARK PURPLE VEIN;
DEEP WHITE THROAT

FOUR-SIDED STEM

Purple Loosestrife

Lythrum salicaria ORDER Myrtales ▪ HEIGHT Up to 6 ft (1.8 m)
▪ HABITAT Freshwater, including wetlands, marshes, rivers, streams, and
ditches ▪ RANGE Throughout the United States except Florida; southern
Canada ▪ ZONES 4 to 9 ▪ TYPE Perennial ▪ Eudicot

In the early 1800s, settlers introduced
Purple Loosestrife to North America.
People brought the pretty purple wildflower
to plant in their gardens. Ships brought
the seeds, too. Empty ships filled their
cargo holds with soil so they wouldn't
float too high on the water. There were
seeds in the soil. When the ships dumped
the soil so they could load cargo, the seeds
started growing. Gradually, Purple Loosestrife spread. Today, it ranks as
one of the World Conservation Union's 100 worst invasive species. As
destructive as its presence is, Purple Loosestrife is an attractive wildflower. Its spear-shaped downy leaves have smooth edges. They grow
opposite each other up the plant's woody stalks. Flowers grow on tall
spikes at the top. Each flower has five or six pinkish purple petals. The
petals surround a small yellow center.

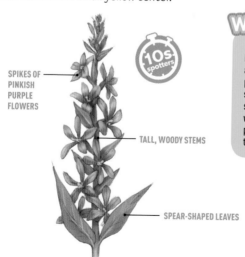

SPIKES OF PINKISH PURPLE FLOWERS

10s. spotters

TALL, WOODY STEMS

SPEAR-SHAPED LEAVES

WILDFLOWER watcher!

Purple Loosestrife is a master
at reproduction. One plant can
produce up to 2.7 million
seeds a year. The seeds are
spread by both wind and
water. Mature plants can also
produce up to 50 shoots from
their rootstocks.

PURPLE LOOSESTRIFE IS ONE OF THE WORLD'S WORST INVASIVE SPECIES.

MANY WILDFLOWERS GROWING IN NORTH AMERICA ARE NATIVE SPECIES. They are adapted to the climate and soil conditions where they naturally occur. Others were introduced, or brought over from somewhere else. Sometimes, as in the case of Red Clover (see page 84), this turns out to be a good thing. But not always. Introduced species can easily become invasive species, which harm the environment around them. Sometimes, their impact is so great that they are classified as noxious weeds. Check out these examples of invasive species.

Common St. John's Wort

Common St. John's Wort (see page 56) was introduced to North America in 1696. It's native to Europe, North Africa, and parts of Asia. Like Purple Loosestrife, Common St. John's Wort is a master of reproduction. One plant can produce up to 23,000 seeds in its lifetime. Many weeds make large numbers of small seeds.

Redstem Stork's Bill

Redstem Stork's Bill (see page 61) is a Eurasian plant that's spread throughout the world. It can spread out to cover large areas with pink-flowering plants. In some states, it's classified as an invasive species.

Queen Anne's Lace

Queen Anne's Lace (see page 134) is an invasive species that can invade the habitats where it grows. Settlers from Europe and Asia brought it to North America in the 1700s. They boiled its roots to use in soups and stews.

10s spotters

Halberdleaf Rosemallow

Hibiscus laevis ORDER **Malvales** · HEIGHT **Up to 6 ft (1.8 m)**
· HABITAT **Fertile, wet soils along streams, rivers, ponds, swamps,
and ditches** · RANGE **Central and Eastern United States; Ontario,
Canada** · ZONES **4 to 9** · TYPE **Perennial** · Eudicot

The Halberdleaf Rosemallow grows up to
six feet (1.8 m) tall and three feet (0.9 m)
wide. Six-inch (15.2-cm)-wide leaves alternate
up its smooth, cylindrical stems. The plant's
flowers are about six inches (15.2 cm) across.
Each flower has five white to pink overlapping
petals with a purple throat. A spiraled column
of stamens sticks out from the middle of the
throat. There's a divided style at the column's
tip. The plant blooms for about one month in late
summer. But each flower lives for only one day.

→ **LOOK FOR THIS**
**THE HALBERDLEAF
ROSEMALLOW'S** leaves are
one of its most distinctive characteristics. They are divided
into three lobes. The middle
lobe is much longer than others.
This makes the leaves look like
a long-handled medieval weapon
called a halberd spear.

10s spotters

Copper Globemallow

Sphaeralcea angustifolia ORDER **Malvales** · HEIGHT **Up to 6 ft (1.8 m)**
· HABITAT **Prairies, plains, pastures, savannas, hillsides, and slopes** · RANGE
Southwestern United States · ZONES **8 to 10** · TYPE **Perennial** · Eudicot

Many wildflowers bloom from the bottom of the
plant to the top. The Copper Globemallow is different.
Its blossoms can open up anywhere along the plant's
tall, hairy stem. Each flower has five petals. The petals

are half an inch (1.3 cm) long. They fit together to form a cup-shaped flower.
The flowers bloom between March and November. And they come in a variety
of colors. Blossoms may be lavender, salmon, red, or pale pink. The Copper
Globemallow's leaves alternate their way up its stem. Like the stem, they
are covered in scratchy, star-shaped hairs. The Copper Globemallow is a
drought-tolerant plant. It may bloom more than once during a rainy year.

Common Marshmallow

Althaea officinalis ORDER **Malvales** • HEIGHT **Up to 6 ft (1.8 m)** • HABITAT **Wet, disturbed areas; along streams, brackish sand, and coastal marshes** • RANGE **Northeastern United States and southeastern Canada** • ZONES **3 to 9** • TYPE **Perennial** • Eudicot

The Common Marshmallow is native to eastern Europe and northern Africa. For more than 2,000 years, people have made medicines out of different parts of the plant. That is likely why it was first introduced to North America. This wildflower has a tall, unbranched stem. Its soft, velvety leaves are oval and have slightly notched edges. They attach to the stem on a short stalk. The pale pink flowers measure about two inches (5.1 cm) across. They bloom in August and September. The Common Marshmallow dies back in the fall. But in the spring, it reappears. Its taproot grows up to a foot (0.3 m) deep in the ground and is used today in medicines.

WILDFLOWER watcher!

The Common Marshmallow's root is full of sap. In the early 19th century, French candymakers used the sap to make the first marshmallows. Getting the sap out of the root must have taken a bit of work. They later replaced the sap with a mixture of egg whites, gelatin, and cornstarch.

PALE PINK FLOWERS

10s spotters

SOFT, VELVETY, OVAL LEAVES WITH SLIGHTLY NOTCHED EDGES

Longbranch Frostweed

Helianthemum canadense ORDER **Malvales**
• HEIGHT **8–24 in (20.3–61 cm)** • HABITAT **Dry, sandy, or rocky open woods and clearings** • RANGE **Eastern United States and southeastern Canada** • ZONES **4 to 6** • TYPE **Perennial** • Eudicot

The Longbranch Frostweed has one main stem. As the wildflower grows, it branches out. Narrow leaves alternate their way up the stem and branches. The leaves look shiny on top and are covered with short, star-shaped and long, unbranched hairs. Only the short, star-shaped hairs grow on the underside of the leaf. Most often, the Longbranch Frostweed produces only one flower. It grows at the tip of the main stem. The flower has five bright yellow petals and 10 or more stamens with orange tips. The flower only lasts for one day. Later, clusters of petal-less flowers grow on the leaf axils and at the tips of the branches. These budlike structures are self-pollinating and produce lots of seeds.

NAME GAME

In late fall sap oozes from cracks in the Longbranch Frostweed's stem. It forms ice crystals as it freezes. That's why this wildflower has "Frostweed" in its common name.

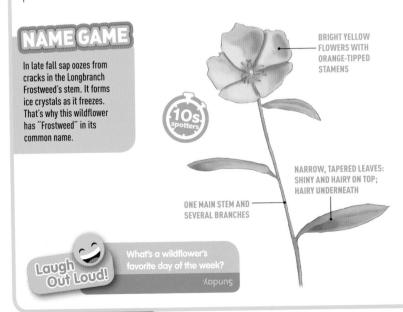

BRIGHT YELLOW FLOWERS WITH ORANGE-TIPPED STAMENS

10s spotters

NARROW, TAPERED LEAVES: SHINY AND HAIRY ON TOP; HAIRY UNDERNEATH

ONE MAIN STEM AND SEVERAL BRANCHES

Laugh Out Loud!
What's a wildflower's favorite day of the week?
Sunday.

Rocky Mountain Beeplant

Cleome serrulata ORDER Brassicales • HEIGHT 4–5 ft
(1.2–1.5 m) • HABITAT Prairies, open woods, and
disturbed sites • RANGE All but southeastern United States;
southern Canada • ZONES 3 to 10 • TYPE Annual • Eudicot

The Rocky Mountain Beeplant has a few
other common names. Two of them are
Stinkweed and Stinking Clover. How does
such an attractive plant get such stinky
names? One whiff and you'll understand.
This wildflower has a most unpleasant odor.
Stench aside, it's a very showy and attractive
wildflower. Leaves divided into three leaflets
alternate their way up its tall, branched stems.
At the end of each stem are fluffy clusters
of compact reddish purple flowers. Each
flower has four petals and sepals and six long
stamens. The flowers bloom from May to
September. When they die back, the fruits
appear. And these fruits are not to be outdone
by the flowers! They are four-inch (10.2-cm)-
long pods that droop from long stems.

WILDFLOWER *watcher!*

Rocky Mountain Beeplant flowers
produce lots of nectar. That's why
they are so great at attracting
bees. They also attract butterflies,
wasps, and hummingbirds.

10s spotters

CLUSTERS
OF REDDISH
PURPLE
FLOWERS

TALL, BRANCHED STEMS

LEAVES DIVIDED INTO
THREE LEAFLETS

True **or** False

**Native Americans
painted with the Rocky
Mountain Beeplant.**
True. They boiled the
plant, removed the woody
parts, and boiled it again.
It turned into a black dye.
They used the dye to
decorate their pottery.

**Livestock like to eat
the Rocky Mountain
Beeplant.**
False. Livestock avoid this
wildflower. The smell
keeps them away.

Yellow Spiderflower

Cleome lutea • ORDER **Brassicales** • HEIGHT **1–3 ft (0.3–0.9 m)** • HABITAT **River bottoms, stream banks, sandy flats, and desert plains** • RANGE **Western United States** • ZONES **3 to 10** • TYPE **Annual** • Eudicot

The Yellow Spiderflower can have one or more stems. The stems branch out, particularly in the upper part of the plant. A crowd of yellow flowers grows at the top of each stem. Each flower has four petals, four sepals, and six stamens. This wildflower has a few traits that help it survive. For one, it has a deep taproot. That's important for plants growing in deserts and on semidesert plains. Deep taproots help them reach water. In addition, this plant can pollinate itself. Toward the end of the day, the stamens coil inward. This causes the anthers and pollen to make contact with the stigma.

WILDFLOWER watcher!

The Yellow Spiderflower can pollinate itself, but that's not always necessary. Bees, wasps, and butterflies pollinate it, too. In fact, more than 140 species of native bees have been observed getting nectar or pollen from this wildflower.

YELLOW FLOWERS WITH FOUR PETALS, FOUR SEPALS, AND SIX STAMENS

LEAVES DIVIDED INTO 3–7 LEAFLETS

Laugh Out Loud!

What is Peter Parker's favorite kind of flower?

The Yellow Spiderflower.

Cutleaf Toothwort

Cardamine concatenata ORDER **Brassicales** ◦ HEIGHT **8–15 in (20.3–38.1 cm)** ◦ HABITAT **Rich deciduous forests and wooded slopes** ◦ RANGE **Eastern United States and southeastern Canada** ◦ ZONES **3 to 8** ◦ TYPE **Perennial** ◦ Eudicot

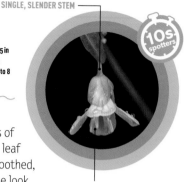

SINGLE, SLENDER STEM

WHITE, BELL-SHAPED FLOWERS

The Cutleaf Toothwort has a single, slender stem. Its leaves grow in spirals of three at the bottom of the stem. Each leaf is cut into three lobes. The lobes are toothed, or deeply notched. That makes one lobe look like it has five different parts. The Cutleaf Toothwort's flowers grow in a floppy cluster at the top. Buds are light pink. The bell-shaped flowers are white and may have pink or lavender tips. The flower's fruits are elongated seedpods. Each pod contains a single row of 10 to 14 small, brown, flat, oval seeds.

WILDFLOWER watcher!

The Cutleaf Toothwort is a native species in all of the eastern states. Yet many people will never see its flowers. That's because this wildflower completes its entire reproductive cycle in just one month.

Western Wallflower

CLUSTER OF FLOWERS AT TOP OF STEM

FOUR-PETALED ORANGE OR YELLOW FLOWERS

Erysimum capitatum
ORDER **Brassicales** ◦ HEIGHT **1–2 ft (0.3–0.6 m)** ◦ HABITAT **Plains, foothills, and high-elevation coniferous forests** ◦ RANGE **Western, central, and mid-Atlantic United States; Alaska** ◦ ZONES **3 to 7** ◦ TYPE **Biennial/Perennial** ◦ Eudicot

A round head of bright orange or yellow flowers grows at the top of the Western Wallflower. Each flower has four petals and measures about an inch (2.5 cm) across. Depending on the length of the growing season and amount of precipitation, the Western Wallflower may be a biennial or perennial wildflower. As a biennial, it usually produces flowers the first year rather than the second. The leaves, stems, and fruits appear to be covered with flat white hairs. The "hairs" are actually tiny stalks that lie flat.

Hairy Rockcress

Arabis hirsuta **ORDER Brassicales** ◦ **HEIGHT 8–25 in (20.3– 63.5 cm)** ◦ **HABITAT Sandy or rocky cliffs, bluffs, and prairies** ◦ **RANGE Most of United States; throughout Canada** ◦ **ZONES 5 to 7** ◦ **TYPE Annual/Biennial/Perennial** ◦ Eudicot

The Hairy Rockcress usually has one stem, but sometimes it has two or three. The stem can grow up to two feet (0.6 m) high. Its bottom half is covered with short, coarse hairs. The top half is smooth. A ring of oblong, hairy leaves grows around the plant's base. These lower leaves can be up to four inches (10.2 cm) long. Upper leaves are smaller. They clasp, or encircle, the stem. At the very top of the stem, the plant produces a cluster of tiny pink, cream-colored, or white flowers. The flowers bloom from May to July. Then the seedpods appear. They are long, flat, and hairless. They stand straight up on the stem.

True or False

Some members of the Mustard family have developed into food plants.
True. Cauliflower, radish, and turnip are all members of the Mustard family.

The seedpods of a plant in the Mustard family are called "siliques."
True. One seedpod is a silique. Remember that word the next time you play Scrabble!

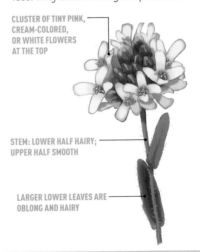

CLUSTER OF TINY PINK, CREAM-COLORED, OR WHITE FLOWERS AT THE TOP

STEM: LOWER HALF HAIRY; UPPER HALF SMOOTH

LARGER LOWER LEAVES ARE OBLONG AND HAIRY

Laugh Out Loud!

Why did the mustard plant cross the road?

To ketchup with his friends.

Western Tansymustard

Descurainia pinnata ORDER **Brassicales**
◦ HEIGHT **4–28 in (10.2–71.1 cm)** ◦ HABITAT **Sandy or gravelly areas with disturbed soil, such as roadsides and along railroad tracks** ◦ RANGE **Throughout the United States and Canada** ◦ ZONES **3 to 10** ◦ TYPE **Annual/Biennial/Perennial** ◦ Eudicot

The Western Tansymustard's leaves are the inspiration for its scientific name, *Descurainia pinnata*. The leaves are divided into many small lobes. Each lobe has a pointed tip. Botanists would say these leaves are divided pinnately. This means that the leaves are shaped like feathers. The leaves and the stems on this wildflower are covered with very short hairs. Flat-topped clusters of yellow flowers grow at the tip of each stem. These flowers are tiny. The spoon-shaped petals are less than one-eighth of an inch (0.3 cm) across. When the seedpods, or siliques, appear, they grow at 60-degree angles from the stem. Each club-shaped seedpod contains two rows of seeds. There are 10 to 20 seeds in each row.

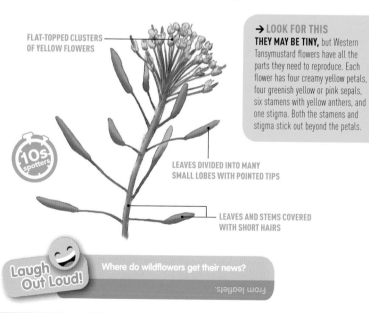

FLAT-TOPPED CLUSTERS OF YELLOW FLOWERS

LEAVES DIVIDED INTO MANY SMALL LOBES WITH POINTED TIPS

LEAVES AND STEMS COVERED WITH SHORT HAIRS

10s spotters

→ LOOK FOR THIS

THEY MAY BE TINY, but Western Tansymustard flowers have all the parts they need to reproduce. Each flower has four creamy yellow petals, four greenish yellow or pink sepals, six stamens with yellow anthers, and one stigma. Both the stamens and stigma stick out beyond the petals.

Laugh Out Loud! Where do wildflowers get their news?

From leaflets.

FRECKLED VIOLETS GROW IN A GARDEN.

PETALS ARE AN IMPORTANT PART OF A FLOWER.

Their main function is to attract pollinators. Some petals even have spots and stripes that guide pollinators right where the flower needs them to go to pollinate. What petals look like depends on the type of flower. Petals grow in many different shapes, colors, and sizes. They come in different patterns, too. Here are a few examples.

Black-eyed Susan

A ring of petals surrounds the rounded dome in the middle of a Black-eyed Susan (see page 131). Like many other wildflowers, it's shaped like a disk.

Hoary Skullcap

Some flowers have lips! The Hoary Skullcap's (see page 123) upper lip is shaped like a hood. Its sides curl back. Its bigger, broader lower lip has a white patch in the flower's throat.

Pickerelweed

Many flowers like Pickerelweed (see page 36) grow in spikes. The individual flowers are tiny. You have to look closely to see the pattern their petals make.

Fire Pink

Fire Pink's (see page 87) five petals grow in the shape of a star. The tip of each petal has a deep notch in it.

FEATHERY SEEDS WITH LONG, PINKISH GRAY TAILS

Old Man's Whiskers

Geum triflorum ORDER **Rosales** · HEIGHT **6–18 in (15.2–45.7 cm)** · HABITAT **Dry, open woodlands; prairies; open slopes; mountain meadows** · RANGE **Northern and western United States; throughout Canada** · ZONES **3 to 7** · TYPE **Perennial** · Eudicot

Old Man's Whiskers is an interesting and attractive wildflower. Hairy, blue-green, fernlike leaves grow at its bottom. Reddish purple, bell-shaped flowers hang in groups of three from its top. As the flowers die back, the styles grow to about two inches (5.1 cm) long. They turn into a cluster of feathery seeds with long, pinkish gray tails. These tails have earned this wildflower a host of common names. Depending on where you live, you might know it as the Torch Flower, Long-Plumed Purple Avens, Prairie Smoke, Lion's Beard, or Old Man's Whiskers.

WILDFLOWER *watcher!*

Old Man's Whiskers often produce flowers during their second year. But the petals on these young plants are nearly closed. Bumblebees can damage the flowers when they force their way in, searching for nectar.

Bride's Feathers

CLUSTER OF FLOWERS AT TOP OF STEM

Aruncus dioicus ORDER **Rosales** · HEIGHT **4–6 ft (1.2–1.8 m)** · HABITAT **Damp, fertile woodlands, mountainous areas** · RANGE **Eastern, central, and West Coast of United States; Alaska; southeastern and western Canada** · ZONES **4 to 8** · TYPE **Perennial** · Eudicot

Bride's Feathers, also known as Goat's Beard, is a tall, bushy plant with lots of dark green leaves. Feathery spikes of small ivory flowers grow at the top of each stem. These flowers are gender specific. Male flowers, which have many stamens, grow on one plant. Female flowers, which have three pistils each, grow on another. Like many other species in nature, the male flowers have a more eye-catching bloom. This wildflower blooms in midsummer. It usually grows alone and not in large colonies. Butterflies are its primary pollinators.

Dwarf Cinquefoil

YELLOW FLOWERS WITH FIVE PETALS

FIVE SEPALS

Potentilla canadensis ORDER **Rosales** ◦ HEIGHT **2–6 in (5.1–15.2 cm)** ◦ HABITAT **Dry, open soil, open woodlands** ◦ RANGE **Eastern United States to Texas; southeastern Canada** ◦ ZONES **4 to 8** ◦ TYPE **Perennial** ◦ **Eudicot**

The Dwarf Cinquefoil is a low-growing plant. Its silvery, hairy stems produce runners that can grow up to 20 inches (50.8 cm) long. It can spread out to form a large mat that carpets the ground. When it comes to flower parts, five is the magic number for this wildflower. Its leaves are divided into five wedge-shaped parts. Its bright yellow flowers have five petals. And these petals rise above a ring of five green sepals. The flowers grow from the axis of the lowest leaf. They bloom between March and June.

True or False

The Dwarf Cinquefoil grows in fertile soil.
False. Dwarf Cinquefoil is actually an indicator that the soil in an area is very poor.

The word "cinquefoil" means five leaves in French.
True.

Silverweed

SPEAR-SHAPED LEAFLETS WITH JAGGED EDGES

SMALL YELLOW FLOWERS, FIVE PETALS, AND MANY STAMENS

WHITE, SILKY HAIRS ON THE BOTTOM OF EACH LEAFLET

Argentina anserina ORDER **Rosales** ◦ HEIGHT **6–9 in (15.2–22.9 cm)** ◦ HABITAT **Coastlines, meadows, moist riverbanks** ◦ RANGE **Northern and western United States; Alaska; throughout Canada** ◦ ZONES **5 to 8** ◦ TYPE **Perennial** ◦ **Eudicot**

Silverweed produces a flat ring of long runners. Most of the runners are covered with leaves. These leaves are divided into 5 to 11 pairs of leaflets. The leaflets are spear-shaped and have extremely jagged edges. They are attached directly opposite from each other on the stem. Their upper surface is yellowish green to dark green in color. But the underside looks silver because it is covered with white, silky hairs. Small yellow flowers grow from separate stalks. Each flower has five petals and many stamens.

→ LOOK FOR THIS

SILVERWEED reproduces in several different ways. Its seeds have a corky outer coating. This allows them to float on water. And they're so small that they are easily blown about in the wind. In addition, this wildflower's taproot branches out. As the root system grows, new shoots emerge, and they create colonies of plants identical to the original one.

RED BERRIES

Wild Strawberry

Fragaria virginiana ORDER **Rosales** ▪ HEIGHT **4–7 in (10.2–17.8 cm)**
▪ HABITAT **Fields, prairies, and woodland edges** ▪ RANGE **Throughout the United States and Canada** ▪ ZONES **5 to 9** ▪ TYPE **Perennial** ▪ Eudicot

WHITE FLOWERS WITH YELLOW STAMENS

LEAVES DIVIDED INTO THREE PARTS

HAIRY LEAF PETIOLES AND FLOWER STALKS

Wild Strawberries aren't tall plants, but their long, stout runners can spread out indefinitely. This can result in huge colonies. The Wild Strawberry plant has hairy leaf petioles and hairy flower stalks. Each leaf petiole produces one leaf. That leaf is divided into three parts. Each flower stalk produces a cluster of small flowers. The flowers have five silky petals and up to 25 yellow stamens. Starting in early summer, this plant produces sweet, fleshy, red berries.

WILDFLOWER watcher!

Store-bought strawberries are a combination of *Fragaria virginiana*, which is native to North America, and *Fragaria chiloensis*. That species is native to coastal South America, and to the western coast of North America. The North American strawberry provides the sweet taste. The South American fruit adds a lot of size. Leave the Wild Strawberries for the animals to eat.

Laugh Out Loud!

Why was the strawberry disappointed on its birthday?

It got a shortcake.

Appalachian Barren Strawberry

Waldsteinia fragarioides ORDER **Rosales**
▪ HEIGHT **4–6 in (10.2–15.2 cm)** ▪ HABITAT **Moist to dry woodlands; pine forests** ▪ RANGE **Eastern United States and southeastern Canada**
▪ ZONES **4 to 7** ▪ TYPE **Perennial** ▪ Eudicot

It can be easy to confuse the Appalachian Barren Strawberry with Wild Strawberry plants. The two species grow to the same height. They both spread via runners. Their flowers and leaves grow on separate stalks. And their leaves are both divided into three wedge-shaped leaflets. But that's where the similarities end. Appalachian Barren Strawberry flowers are yellow, not white. Its single-seeded fruit doesn't open and isn't edible. The Appalachian Barren Strawberry is, however, an excellent source of ground cover. And it grows best in shady, moist wooded areas.

YELLOW FLOWERS WITH YELLOW STAMENS

Drummond's Mountain-Avens

Dryas drummondii ORDER **Rosales** • HEIGHT **Up to 8 in (20.3 cm)**
• HABITAT **High mountain ridges; gravelly slopes, stream banks, and foothills**
• RANGE **Northwestern United States and Alaska; throughout Canada**
• ZONES **2 to 7** • TYPE **Perennial** • Eudicot

YELLOW FLOWERS WITH 8–10 PETALS

10s spotters

DARK GREEN CALYX COVERED WITH DARK BROWN, SHAGGY HAIRS

Drummond's Mountain-Avens doesn't grow very tall or very fast. But it can spread to cover an area about three feet (0.9 m) wide. As it spreads, it forms a mat of oval, leathery leaves with scalloped edges. The leaves are dark green on top and have woolly white hairs on the bottom. The leaves keep their color throughout winter. But they wither away in spring when the plant grows new leaves. Single flowers grow on top of two-to-eight-inch (5.1–20.3 cm) stems. The petals are encased in a dark green calyx that is covered with dark brown, shaggy hairs.

→ **LOOK FOR THIS**
THE PETALS ON DRUMMOND'S MOUNTAIN-AVENS don't spread out as they grow. Instead, they grow straight up. This makes it look like the flower never fully opens. When the flowers wilt, the fruits develop. The seeds look fluffy and feathery because they're covered with long yellow hairs.

Queen of the Prairie

10s spotters

Filipendula rubra ORDER **Rosales** • HEIGHT **3–6 ft (0.9–1.8 m)** • HABITAT **Moist meadows and prairies; bogs** • RANGE **Northeastern quarter of United States and southeastern Canada** • ZONES **3 to 8** • TYPE **Perennial** • Eudicot

CLUSTER OF PINK FLOWERS AT TOP OF STEM

WILDFLOWER watcher!

The cluster of flowers on top of a Queen of the Prairie can be up to eight inches (20.3 cm) across. Individual flowers are just one-third of an inch (0.8 cm) wide. Each flower has five pink petals and numerous white stamens with pink anthers.

From a distance, Queen of the Prairie flowers in full bloom could be mistaken for a tuft of pink cotton candy. This tall, robust perennial produces large sprays of small pink flowers. Each flower has many stamens. When the flowers open, the stamens turn the cluster into a feathery pink mass. The wildflower's leaves are just as showy. The yellowish green leaves can be two to three feet (0.6–0.9 m) long. Each one is deeply cut into seven to nine lobes.

Red Clover

Trifolium pratense ORDER **Fabales** • HEIGHT **0.5–2 in (1.3–5.1 cm)** • HABITAT **Meadows, fields, lawns, roadsides, riverbanks, valleys, and plains** • RANGE **Throughout the United States and Canada** • ZONES **3 to 8** • TYPE **Biennial/Perennial** • Eudicot

Red Clover is commonly found in meadows, vacant lots, and other areas that aren't mowed very often. When in bloom, it's easy to spot. Each plant has several rounded dull pink to rosy purple flower heads. If you smell the flower heads, you'll be greeted with a mild honeylike fragrance. If you look closely at the heads, you'll see that each one is actually made up of lots of little flowers. These tiny flowers are pea-shaped. That means they have five petals, including a broad banner petal, two wing petals, and two keels. The flower heads grow at the top of a hollow, hairy stem.

→ **LOOK FOR THIS**
EACH RED CLOVER LEAF is divided into three oval leaflets. The leaflets are green and have a white or light green V-pattern right in the middle. Each leaflet can be up to two inches (5.1 cm) long and three-quarters of an inch (1.9 cm) wide.

WILDFLOWER watcher!

Although Red Clover is found throughout North America, it is not a native plant. It was brought over from Europe. Farmers planted Red Clover so they could feed it to their animals as hay. In addition, it's an excellent cover crop. It prevents other weeds from growing. And its roots produce lots of nitrogen, which improves the soil.

DULL PINK TO ROSY PURPLE FLOWER HEADS

HOLLOW, HAIRY STEM

LEAVES DIVIDED INTO THREE OVAL LEAFLETS

Purple Milkvetch

CLUSTERS OF PINK, LAVENDER, OR PURPLE FLOWERS

Astragalus agrestis ORDER **Fabales** · HEIGHT **6–12 in (15.2–30.5 cm)** · HABITAT **Moist meadows and prairies and on cool, brushy slopes** · RANGE **Upper Midwest and western United States; throughout Canada** · ZONES **3 to 8** · TYPE **Perennial** · Eudicot

FEATHERLIKE LEAVES   SOFT GREEN STEM

Purple Milkvetch grows in patches in cool, moist meadows and prairies. This is a soft, green plant. Its stems can grow up to 12 inches (30.5 cm) tall. But they're so weak that they often lean on other plants for support. Its leaves are featherlike and alternate their way up the stem. The flowers grow in tightly packed clusters at the tips of leaf axils. Up to 20 pink, lavender, or purple flowers may be in one cluster. The flowers on the outside of the cluster bloom first.

CLUSTERS OF DEEP LAVENDER FLOWERS

Showy Locoweed

Oxytropis splendens ORDER **Fabales** · HEIGHT **4–16 in (10.2–40.6 cm)** · HABITAT **Prairies and plains** · RANGE **Southern Rocky Mountains and northern Great Plains in the United States; throughout Canada** · ZONES **2 to 8** · TYPE **Perennial** · Eudicot

DANGER!

Locoweeds are also called Crazyweeds. And many of them, including the Showy Locoweed, are poisonous if eaten by humans or animals. If a cow eats the wildflower, the toxins may even be passed on to humans through milk. The condition is called locoism.

Numerous featherlike leaves grow from the base of the Showy Locoweed. The leaves are about 10 inches (25.4 cm) long. They are divided into small, hairy, grayish green leaflets. The leaflets grow in spiraled groups with up to five leaflets in each group. The wildflower's stems have no leaves. Instead, they are covered with long, silky, silvery hairs. A spike of deep lavender flowers grows at the top of each stem. These spikes are crowded, with between 20 to 80 flowers growing on each. The flowers bloom between June and August.

Laugh Out Loud!

Knock, knock. Who's there? Peas. Peas who? Peas open the door! It's cold outside!

SPIKE OF
VIOLET FLOWERS

SILKY, SILVERY HAIRS
ON STEMS AND LEAVES

ONE OR MORE STEMS

Silvery Lupine

Lupinus argenteus ORDER **Fabales** ▪ HEIGHT **1–2 ft (0.3–0.6 m)** ▪ HABITAT **Stream valleys, dry roadsides, prairies, open forest, and woodlands** ▪ RANGE **Western United States and southwestern Canada** ▪ ZONES **3 to 8** ▪ TYPE **Perennial** ▪ Eudicot

The Silvery Lupine is likely named for the silky hairs that cover its stems and leaves. The hairs give the wildflower a silvery sheen. This plant can have one or more stems. Palmlike leaves grow opposite each other on the stems. Each leaf is divided into six to nine leaflets. A spike of violet flowers grows at the top. Like all plants in the pea family, these flowers have five petals: a broad banner petal on top, two smaller wing petals, and two elongated keels at the bottom.

→ LOOK FOR THIS
THERE'S USUALLY A WHITE SPOT on the banner petal of a Silvery Lupine. This spot attracts pollinators, like bees. As the flower ages, the spot turns red. This tells bees to move on to another flower. Not only does this keep bees from visiting flowers with limited nectar, it also ensures that newer pollen is collected and spread to other flowers.

Littleleaf Sensitive-briar

Mimosa microphylla ORDER **Fabales** ▪ HEIGHT **Up to 3 ft (0.9 m)** ▪ HABITAT **Sandhills, prairies, ravines, open woodlands, and roadsides** ▪ RANGE **Southeastern United States, Texas, Kansas, and Illinois** ▪ ZONES **6 to 11** ▪ TYPE **Perennial** ▪ Eudicot

FLOWERS LOOK LIKE
TINY PINK POM-POMS

FEATHERY LEAVES THAT
CLOSE IF TOUCHED

The Littleleaf Sensitive-briar's stem may be weak, but it's armed with little, prickly thorns. So if this wild-flower is around, you'd better watch your step. It doesn't grow up. It sprawls along the ground. One easy way to spot it is to look for the flowers. The Littleleaf Sensitive-briar's flowers look like tiny pink pom-poms. And the feathery leaflets on either side of its leaves close if you touch them. They stay folded together for up to five minutes before they open again. This may be a way for them to avoid being eaten.

NAME GAME

The Latin word *mimo* means "mimic" or "actor." The Greek word *micr* means "small." and the Greek word *phyll* means "a leaf." Put those words together and you've got *Mimosa microphylla*, the scientific name of the Littleleaf Sensitive-briar. It's also a perfect description of this wildflower.

Fire Pink

Silene virginica ORDER **Carophyllales** • HEIGHT **12–18 in (30.5–45.7 cm)** • HABITAT **Rich woodlands and rocky slopes** • RANGE **Eastern United States; Ontario, Canada** • ZONES **4 to 8** • TYPE **Perennial** • Eudicot

The Fire Pink is proof that wildflowers don't have to be large to stand out. Its flowers are no more than 1.5 inches (3.8 cm) across. But they have five flaming red petals with distinct notches at the end. This makes them hard to miss. The petals and the sepals grow together around a long, sticky tube in the center of the flower. The flowers grow in loose clusters at the top of a long, slender, sticky stem. Lower leaves are shaped like spatulas. They're broader at the tip than they are near the stem. Stem leaves are slightly longer and spear-shaped. They grow in pairs opposite each other up the flower's stem. The stems are also sticky. Nobody has studied this yet, but scientists think that the sticky stems may help to prevent insects from eating the plants.

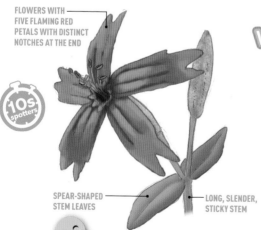

FLOWERS WITH FIVE FLAMING RED PETALS WITH DISTINCT NOTCHES AT THE END

10s spotters

SPEAR-SHAPED STEM LEAVES

LONG, SLENDER, STICKY STEM

WILDFLOWER watcher!

Catchfly is another common name often used for the Fire Pink. That's because small insects get trapped in the long, sticky tube in the center of the flower. But flies aren't this wildflower's primary pollinator. That honor belongs to the Ruby-throated Hummingbird. The hummingbirds are attracted to the bright red flowers.

Laugh Out Loud! What's it called when a fly lands on a Fire Pink flower?

A sticky situation.

Alpine Golden Buckwheat

Eriogonum flavum ORDER Carophyllales ◦ HEIGHT 2–8 in (5.1–20.3 cm) ◦ HABITAT Dry grasslands, shrublands, and rocky slopes at moderate to high elevations ◦ RANGE Upper Great Plains and northwestern United States; western and south-central Canada; Alaska ◦ ZONES 2 to 6 ◦ TYPE Biennial/Perennial ◦ Eudicot

Alpine Golden Buckwheat is one of the many species of wild buckwheat found in North America. This perennial grows from a deep taproot. It has a stout, hairy stem that branches out to form mats of oblong leaves. Although green on top, woolly hairs make the leaves appear white underneath. Between late May and mid-July, the golden yellow flowers bloom. Alpine Golden Buckwheat flowers grow in umbrella-shaped clusters. Each flower is less than a quarter inch (0.6 cm) across. Both the stamens and styles are longer than the petals. After the flowers wilt, small brown seeds form. Because these plants grow at higher altitudes, most seeds are spread downhill. Any seeds that go uphill are blown there by the wind.

WILDFLOWER watcher!

Native Americans used Alpine Golden Buckwheat flowers to tan buffalo hides. They also mashed up the roots to make earplugs. Children ate the sweet roots as a snack.

MAKE THIS!

"Tan" a Paper Towel

Round up: aluminum foil, white paper towels, a wooden mallet, and flowers of different colors

1. Lay a sheet of aluminum foil on a flat surface.
2. Lay the flowers on top of the foil. Place some flowers by themselves and layer others.
3. Put the paper towel on top of the flowers and begin hammering.
4. Pigment from the flowers should have seeped through the paper towel.
5. Hammer harder or softer where flowers overlap. Do the colors mix? Observe how the flower pigment helps you create a design.

GOLDEN YELLOW FLOWERS GROWING IN UMBRELLA-SHAPED CLUSTERS

STOUT, HAIRY STEM

10s spotters

Threadleaf Sundew

Drosera filiformis ORDER **Carophyllales** ▪ HEIGHT **6–12 in (15.2–30.5 cm)** ▪ HABITAT **Wet, sandy coastal areas** ▪ RANGE **Atlantic Coast in United States and Nova Scotia, Canada** ▪ ZONES **6 to 9** ▪ TYPE **Perennial** ▪ Eudicot

The Threadleaf Sundew produces small lavender-pink flowers. They're quite dainty and look perfectly inviting to insects. But any insects that visit this plant aren't likely to escape. That's because of the leaves. This plant has dozens of long, upright, threadlike leaves. Each leaf is covered with tiny red tentacles. And each tentacle secretes a moist, sticky substance. If an insect lands on a leaf, it's stuck. For the next four to six days, enzymes in the leaf digest the insect. The plant sends the nutrients to its roots. The plants grow in nutrient-poor soil so insects are an important nutritional resource.

LONG, UPRIGHT, THREADLIKE LEAVES COVERED IN TINY RED TENTACLES

WILDFLOWER watcher!

The Threadleaf Sundew must go dormant to survive winter. The plant produces a small, brown, dormant bud just at or below the surface, called a hibernaculum. When warmer temperatures return, the plant grows again from the hibernaculum.

Dwarf Sundew

HAIRS ON LEAVES SECRETE CLEAR, STICKY LIQUID

DELICATE RED STEM WITH SEVERAL BUDS

SMALL FLOWERS WITH FIVE PALE PINK PETALS

RING OF GREEN-AND-RED PADDLE-SHAPED LEAVES

Drosera brevifolia ORDER **Carophyllales** ▪ HEIGHT **Up to 6 in (15.2 cm)** ▪ HABITAT **Open, sandy woods** ▪ RANGE **Southeastern United States to Texas** ▪ ZONES **6 to 9** ▪ TYPE **Annual/Perennial** ▪ Eudicot

The Dwarf Sundew is a small plant. It typically measures just one to two inches (2.5–5 cm) across. And when its pale pink flowers bloom, they shoot up just six inches (15.2 cm). But small plants can still be deadly to insects. The Dwarf Sundew's spoon-shaped leaves form a carnivorous ring on the ground. The upper surface of these green-and-red leaves is covered with hairs that secrete a clear sticky liquid. When insects touch the liquid, they stick. Then enzymes in the leaves digest the insects.

WILDFLOWER watcher!

The Dwarf Sundew does not go dormant in the winter. It grows until it flowers. Once the flowers are gone, the plant dies. If something happens and the flowers don't bloom, the plant will live another year.

WHITE PETALS WITH DARK PINK VEINS

Carolina Springbeauty

Claytonia caroliniana ORDER **Carophyllales** ▪ HEIGHT **4–12 in (10.2–30.5 cm)** ▪ HABITAT **Rich open woodlands** ▪ RANGE **Eastern United States and southeastern Canada** ▪ ZONES **5 to 9** ▪ TYPE **Perennial** ▪ Eudicot

The Carolina Springbeauty is an early spring wildflower. It typically blooms between March and June. But it can appear as early as February in some places. This low-growing wildflower has spatula-shaped leaves at its base. And one pair of leaves grows halfway up the stem. These stem leaves are oval or spear-shaped, and they taper inward near the stem. A loose cluster of decorative flowers grows at the tip of the stem. Each flower has five white petals that are lined with dark pink veins.

WILDFLOWER watcher!

The Carolina Springbeauty grows in shady forest areas. Blooming in early spring is an adaptation. It allows the plant to capture as much sunlight as possible before the forest canopy leaves expand and block sunlight.

Lanceleaf Springbeauty

Claytonia lanceolata ORDER **Carophyllales** ▪ HEIGHT **2–6 in (5.1–15.2 cm)** ▪ HABITAT **Moist foothills, mountain meadows and forests, and alpine slopes** ▪ RANGE **Western United States and southwestern Canada** ▪ ZONES **3 to 8** ▪ TYPE **Annual/Perennial** ▪ Eudicot

SLENDER, ERECT STEM

FLOWERS WITH WHITE OR PINK PETALS AND DARK PINK VEINS

WILDFLOWER watcher!

The Lanceleaf Springbeauty grows from an underground tuber. This tuber is an important food source for black bears, grizzly bears, and burrowing rodents. People eat them, too. They taste like potatoes.

The Lanceleaf Springbeauty blooms each spring after the snow melts. The slender, erect stem only gets up to six inches (15.2 cm) tall. And the flowers are about the size of a dime. Each star-shaped flower has five white or pink petals. The petals are lined with dark pink veins and have a yellow spot near their base. Five stamens with pink anthers stick out from the middle. Each plant can produce 15 to 20 flowers, and there can be thousands of them covering patches of ground.

Shoreline Seapurslane

Sesuvium portulacastrum ORDER Carophyllales
- HEIGHT 6–12 in (15.2–30.5 cm) - HABITAT Coastal dunes and beaches
- RANGE Southeastern United States to Texas; Pennsylvania and Hawaii - ZONES 9 to 11 - TYPE Annual - Eudicot

Shoreline Seapurslane is a dense groundcover. It spreads out to form large patches on the ocean side of sand dunes. It stops growing at the point where it reaches the high tide mark. This plant has thick, fleshy leaves and succulent reddish green stems. Its flowers are small, star-shaped, and range from white to pink or purple. Each flower opens for a few hours every day. As long as the temperature remains high enough, the flowers bloom all year long. But this wildflower doesn't produce many flowers. And those that it does have are scattered across the large mat of stems and leaves. Because of this, the flowers aren't always noticed.

WILDFLOWER watcher!

Shoreline Seapurslane is the only plant in the *Sesuvium* genus that is native to Hawaii. On the Hawaiian Islands, it is known as 'Ākulikuli. It grows well there because it is one of the most salt tolerant of all coastal plants.

SMALL STAR-SHAPED FLOWERS

THICK, FLESHY LEAVES

SUCCULENT REDDISH GREEN STEMS

10s spotters

True or False

People eat the Shoreline Seapurslane's leaves.
True. The leaves are very salty, but they're a great source of vitamin C. In the Philippines, pickled leaves are called *dampalit*.

Shoreline Seapurslanes help form sand dunes.
True. Sand catches between the stems and leaves. This builds sand dunes.

LONG, BRANCHING STALKS

Narrowleaf Four O'clock

Mirabilis linearis ORDER **Carophyllales** · HEIGHT **Up to 3 ft (0.9 m)**
· HABITAT **Dry, rocky, or sandy plains, hillsides, and roadsides** · RANGE **Southwestern, Midwest, and Great Plains areas of the United States; south-central Canada**
· ZONES **4 to 9** · TYPE **Perennial** · Eudicot

The Narrowleaf Four O'clock is a native perennial with a deep woody taproot. It can usually be seen blooming from June to September. Its flowers grow in groups of two to four on top of long, branching stalks. They range in color from white to a brilliantly bright magenta. Their color comes from the hairy calyx, not the petals. In fact, members of this family have no petals. The Narrowleaf Four O'clock has blue-gray leaves. The leaves are long and thin, like blades of grass.

HAIRY CALYX RANGING FROM WHITE TO BRIGHT MAGENTA

→ LOOK FOR THIS
FOUR O'CLOCK FLOWERS open in late afternoon. They stay open all night and close again in the morning. That's how this group of flowers got its family name.

Snowball Sand Verbena

Abronia fragrans ORDER **Carophyllales**
· HEIGHT **8–40 in (20.3–101.6 cm)** · HABITAT **Sandy plains, prairies, meadows, pastures, and woodland edges** · RANGE **Most of the western United States**
· ZONES **5 to 8** · TYPE **Perennial** · Eudicot

NAME GAME

The Snowball Sand Verbena is another wildflower with a perfectly matched scientific name. The genus name, *Abronia*, comes from the Greek word *abros*, which means "delicate." The species name, *fragrans*, is a Latin word that means "fragrant."

The Snowball Sand Verbena is sometimes called the Fragrant Verbena. Either name is perfect for this member of the Four O'clock family. This wildflower produces sweet-smelling

BALLS OF TINY WHITE FLOWERS THAT MAY BE TINGED WITH GREEN, LAVENDER, OR PINK

spheres packed with dozens of tiny flowers. The Snowball Sand Verbena's balls of flowers grow at the tips of sticky, hairy, branching stems. Its egg-shaped leaves are covered with sticky hairs, too. This wildflower has a long blooming season, lasting from March to September.

Cactus Apple

YELLOW OR REDDISH ORANGE FLOWERS

Opuntia engelmannii ORDER **Carophyllales** · HEIGHT **Up to 8 ft (2.4 m)** · HABITAT **Deserts, grasslands, woodlands, plains, sandy soils to rocky hillsides** · RANGE **Southwestern United States** · ZONES **8 to 10** · TYPE **Perennial** · Eudicot

The Cactus Apple, also called the Prickly Pear, is a large, spreading cactus. It can grow up to eight feet (2.4 m) tall and branch out just as wide. This cactus has broad, flat green pads. The pads are covered with tiny barbed, white hairs and three-inch (7.6-cm)-long white spines. Between April and July, this cactus's yellow or reddish orange flowers bloom. Each funnel-shaped flower is about three inches (7.6 cm) across. After the flowers wilt, the dark maroon, egg-shaped fruits develop. These fruits are called "tuna" and can be eaten or used to make a drink. The pads can also be cooked, peeled, and eaten as a vegetable, called "nopal."

BROAD, FLAT GREEN PADS WITH BARBED HAIRS AND LONG SPINES

DANGER!

The spines on a cactus are actually modified leaves. Their shape conserves water and helps protect the cactus. But they're very sharp. If you touch a spine, it will hurt!

Nightblooming Cereus

FRILLY, WAXY, WHITE FLOWERS

Peniocereus greggii ORDER **Carophyllales** · HEIGHT **1–8 ft (0.3–2.4 m)** · HABITAT **Flats and washes of low-altitude deserts** · RANGE **Texas, Arizona, and New Mexico** · ZONES **9 to 10** · TYPE **Perennial** · Eudicot

For most of the year, the Nightblooming Cereus looks like a thorny, shriveled up, grayish green stick. It blends in with nearby bushes and is easily overlooked. But when it blooms, it's absolutely spectacular. All of this cactus's flowers bloom on the same night in June.

GRAYISH GREEN, STICKLIKE STEM

They bloom at night to attract moth pollinators. The frilly, waxy, white flowers are about 4.5 inches (11.4 cm) across. The center of each flower is crowded with white stamens and a white style. When the sun rises, the flowers close. Soon after, bright red fruits grow.

LOOKING AT LEAVES

Leaves of Sitka Valerian

The Sitka Valerian's (see page 126) leaves grow opposite from each other on the stem. Other plants have leaves that alternate their way up the stem or grow in a spiral.

COMMON WOOD SORREL

LEAVES ARE AN ESSENTIAL PART OF ANY PLANT.

They use energy from sunlight, carbon dioxide from the air, and water from the soil to make food the plant can use. This process is called photosynthesis. In general, people admire wildflowers for their blooms. They don't seek them out for their leaves. But leaves, like every other part of a flower, can be very interesting. These examples will show you what to look for.

Leaves of Dutchman's Breeches

Some leaves are divided so many times that they look feathery. These are the leaves of the Dutchman's Breeches (see page 45).

Leaves of Cactus Apple

The Cactus Apple (see page 93) looks like it has no leaves. But it does! Its thorns are modified leaves. They protect the plant and help it conserve water.

Leaves of Dwarf Sundew

Some plants, like the Dwarf Sundew (see page 89), have leaves that help them get food. When insects land on the leaves, they get stuck. Then the leaf digests the insects.

OVAL, HAIRLESS LEAVES WITH WAVY EDGES

GOLDEN ORANGE CORNUCOPIA-SHAPED FLOWERS WITH REDDISH BROWN SPOTS

Common Jewelweed

Impatiens capensis ORDER **Ericales** • HEIGHT **2–5 ft (0.6–1.5 m)** • HABITAT **Shaded wetlands** • RANGE **Eastern half and northwest of United States; throughout Canada** • ZONES **2 to 11** • TYPE **Annual** • Eudicot

The Common Jewelweed is also called the Spotted Touch-me-not because of its flowers. Shaped like tiny cornucopias, they're golden orange and have reddish brown spots. The flowers dangle from thin leaf stalks. The stalks are attached to shiny green, rounded stems. This wildflower can grow quite tall, but its stems are weak and break easily. When they do, they release the watery substance within. Native Americans used this plant juice to treat poison ivy, stinging nettle, and insect bites. Scientific studies show that it is also effective for treating fungus infections like athlete's foot.

NAME GAME

There are two possible reasons why this wildflower is called a Jewelweed. One is the brightly colored flowers. They dangle from the stems like jewels on a necklace. The other is the leaves. Water from dew or rain beads up to form tiny droplets on the leaves that sparkle in the sun like jewels.

→ LOOK FOR THIS

TOUCH-ME-NOTS have slender seed capsules filled with tiny seeds. If anything touches a ripe seed capsule, it will suddenly split open. It sends an explosive shower of seeds out in all directions. That's why this family of flowers is called Touch-me-nots.

SOFT, LIGHT GREEN STEMS

Pale Touch-me-not

Impatiens pallida ORDER **Ericales** • HEIGHT **3–6 ft (0.9–1.8 m)** • HABITAT **Wet woods and meadows** • RANGE **Eastern United States and southeastern Canada** • ZONES **3 to 8** • TYPE **Annual** • Eudicot

The Pale Touch-me-not is a tall annual with soft, light green stems. It blooms from midsummer to early fall. The downward-facing flowers on its branches grow in small clusters. They are pale yellow and sometimes have reddish brown spots on them. Each flower has five petals and three sepals. The petals and the lower sepal fuse together to form a tube at the back of the flower. Inside that tube there's a downward curving nectar spur. That nectar attracts pollinators, including the Ruby-throated Hummingbird and bumblebees.

SMALL CLUSTERS OF PALE YELLOW FLOWERS THAT MAY HAVE REDDISH BROWN SPOTS

Scarlet Gilia

Ipomopsis aggregata • ORDER **Ericales** • HEIGHT **1–3 ft (0.3–0.9)** • HABITAT **Dry, rocky slopes; lightly wooded areas; grasslands and open forests** • RANGE **Western United States and southwestern Canada** • ZONES **2 to 11** • TYPE **Biennial/Perennial** • Eudicot

The Scarlet Gilia is a common wildflower in the western United States. Even before the flowers appear, the leaves make this plant easy to recognize. They grow in a ring on the ground. They are very finely cut and look silver because they are speckled with fine white hairs. Some leaves also grow up the stem. The flowers, which bloom between May and October, are unmistakable. Each flower has five petals. The petals fuse together to form a tube that is two to three inches (5–7.6 cm) long. They flare out at the end. Most often the flowers are bright red. But there are plants with lighter shades of pink or even white at higher elevations.

WILDFLOWER watcher!

Long-beaked or long-tongued animals pollinate the tube-shaped Scarlet Gilia flowers. But which animals come depends on the flowers' color. Red flowers attract hummingbirds. White flowers attract moths.

BRIGHT RED TUBULAR FLOWERS THAT FLARE OUT AT THE END

True or False

No matter how long it lives, the Scarlet Gilia only flowers once.
True. This wildflower can be a biennial. But it can also be a monocarpic perennial. That means it only flowers once before it dies, although it may take a few years for it to flower.

The Scarlet Gilia has a sweet, fragrant smell.
False. This beautiful wildflower gives off a very unpleasant odor. One of its other common names is the Skunk Flower.

Greek Valerian

Polemonium reptans ORDER **Ericales** • HEIGHT **12–18 in (30.5–45.7 cm)** • HABITAT **Rich, moist woodlands and along streams** • RANGE **Eastern United States and southeastern Canada** • ZONES **3 to 8** • TYPE **Perennial** • Eudicot

LIGHT BLUE-VIOLET BELL-SHAPED FLOWERS WITH WHITE STAMENS

Greek Valerian plants are so packed with leaves that they may sprawl across the ground. That gives this wildflower a floppy appearance. The stems and petioles vary from light green to red. The feather-shaped leaves have 5 to 15 alternating, oval leaflets. The leaflets are medium green and have smooth edges. Clusters of bell-shaped flowers hang from the stems. Each flower has five light blue-violet petals, five white stamens, and a tube-shaped calyx with five triangular teeth. Greek Valerian, also known as Jacob's Ladder, blooms between April and June.

TUBE-SHAPED FLOWERS WITH PALE CENTERS AND FIVE PINK, RED, PURPLE, WHITE, OR PEACH PETALS

Annual Phlox

Phlox drummondii ORDER **Ericales** • HEIGHT **6–12 in (15.2–30.5 cm)** • HABITAT **Grasslands and open woodlands** • RANGE **Southeastern United States to Texas; Minnesota, Wisconsin, Connecticut, and Vermont; southeastern Canada** • ZONES **2 to 11** • TYPE **Annual** • Eudicot

Annual Phlox has bright green, spear-shaped leaves. Lower leaves grow opposite each other. Upper leaves alternate their way up the stem. Its tube-shaped flowers usually have a pale center. But the five petals may be pink, red, purple, white, or even peach. The flowers grow in tight clusters at the ends of the stems. Annual Phlox blooms in early spring and declines when temperatures increase. Sometimes it flowers again in fall. In cooler climates, it may bloom in summer, too.

Laugh Out Loud!

What is Greek Valerian's favorite movie?

Fantastic Mr. Phlox.

WILDFLOWER watcher!

Annual Phlox is native to central and eastern Texas. But it's a prized "exotic" flower in Europe. Botanist Thomas Drummond, whose name is part of the Latin species name, introduced Annual Phlox to Europe in 1835. About 200 varieties of the flower have been developed from the seeds he collected.

Dark-throated Shooting Star

Dodecatheon pulchellum ORDER **Ericales**
HEIGHT **2-20 in (5.1-50.8 cm)** HABITAT **Stream banks, wet
mountain meadows, and coastal wetlands** RANGE
**Western United States; central and western Canada;
Alaska** ZONES **3 to 7** TYPE **Perennial** Eudicot

Unlike many wildflowers, the
Dark-throated Shooting Star
doesn't use its petals to form a
protective case around its reproductive parts. This wildflower's five
magenta petals flare straight back
toward the stem. Each petal has a large white
spot at its base. A dark purple ring separates
those white spots from a bright yellow tube.
That tube is where the filaments unite at the
flower's center. Their anthers and the style stick
out to create a dark purple tip. The Dark-
throated Shooting Star's flowers grow in clusters at the top of tall, straight stems. One plant
can produce up to 25 flowers. Large, oval leaves
grow at the plant's base.

NAME GAME

The Dark-throated Shooting
Star's common name refers
to its cometlike shape. The
petals, in this case, are the
comet's tail.

**COMET-SHAPED
FLOWERS
WITH MAGENTA
PETALS**

10S
spotters

TALL, STRAIGHT STEMS

True **or** False

**Hummingbirds are the Dark-throated
Shooting Star's primary pollinators.**
False. This wildflower attracts bees. They
buzz-pollinate the flowers. The bees vibrate
their flight muscles, or the muscles that control their wings, hundreds of times a second.
This shakes the pollen from the anthers.

**Native Americans used the Dark-throated
Shooting Star to make eyedrops.**
True. They made eyedrops out of the
leaves. They used the roots to create
an eyewash, too.

Fringed Loosestrife

Lysimachia ciliata ORDER **Ericales** • HEIGHT **1–4 ft (0.3–1.2 m)** • HABITAT **Low, wet deciduous woodlands; prairies, thickets, swamps, and stream banks** • RANGE **Most of the United States, including Alaska; throughout Canada** • ZONES **3 to 9** • TYPE **Perennial** • Eudicot

Fringed Loosestrife has a tall central stem that, on occasion, branches out. Medium-green, spear-shaped leaves grow opposite each other along the stem. The leaf stalks that connect the leaves to the stem are covered with long, noticeable hairs. That's why this wildflower has the word "fringed" in its common name. The Fringed Loosestrife's flowers hang from long pedicels on the upper half of the plant. Each flower has five yellow petals and five stamens. The petals are oval. But like the leaves, they come to a sharp point at the tip. The center of the flower is often red. This coloring draws pollinators toward the creamy yellow stamens and the slender style that are located here.

WILDFLOWER watcher!

The Fringed Loosestrife attracts a very particular pollinator, the Melittid Bee. This small bee is a specialist when it comes to pollination. It only collects floral oil and pollen from plants in the *Lysimachia* genus. The bee feeds the oil and pollen to its larvae.

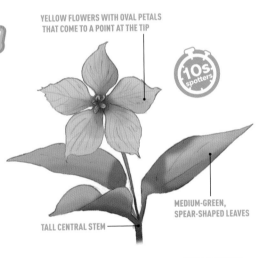

YELLOW FLOWERS WITH OVAL PETALS THAT COME TO A POINT AT THE TIP

10s spotters

MEDIUM-GREEN, SPEAR-SHAPED LEAVES

TALL CENTRAL STEM

Laugh Out Loud!

Why did the primrose read an entire book in one evening?

The plot was very stem-ulating.

Parry's Primrose

FLOWERS WITH FIVE MAGENTA PETALS AND A YELLOW CENTER

Primula parryi ORDER Ericales • HEIGHT 6–20 in (15.2–50.8 cm) • HABITAT Rich, moist woodlands and along streams • RANGE Western United States along the central Rocky Mountain range • ZONES 3 to 5 • TYPE Perennial • Eudicot

RING OF LONG, BROAD, BRIGHT GREEN LEAVES AT THE BASE

LONG, ERECT STEMS

Parry's Primrose stands out for two reasons. First, it is the largest and most eye-catching of all North American Primrose species. And second, it really smells! If you touch the leaves, they emit a rank, skunky stench. This high-alpine wildflower has bright green leaves and intense magenta flowers with yellow centers. The leaves are long, broad, spear-shaped, and leathery. They grow in clumps. The flowers, which start to bloom shortly after the snow melts, grow on long stems. Up to 25 flowers can grow on each stem.

WILDFLOWER watcher!

Many museums have samples of Parry's Primrose in their collections. Even though the samples are pressed and dried, they still stink. The stench is so strong that it can last for years.

WHITE, STAR-SHAPED FLOWERS WITH FIVE TO NINE PETALS (USUALLY SEVEN)

Starflower

SLENDER, LIGHT GREEN STEM

Trientalis borealis ORDER Ericales • HEIGHT less than 8 in (20.3 cm) • HABITAT Shady, moist woodlands, but also areas with dry, sandy, acidic soils • RANGE Eastern and Pacific Coast of United States; most of Canada • ZONES 3 to 7 • TYPE Annual • Eudicot

The Starflower is a low-growing perennial found mostly in shady, moist woods. It has a slender, light green stem. A spiral of leaves grows toward the top of the stem. There may be anywhere from five to nine leaves in the spiral. All of the leaves are spear-shaped and have smooth edges. But some leaves are much larger than others. Up to three star-shaped flowers grow above the spiraled leaves. The flowers have five to nine white, spear-shaped petals. Their stamens have bright yellow tips.

NAME GAME

The Starflower got its common name from the shape of its flowers. Its scientific name refers to its average height and where it typically grows. The genus, *Trientalis*, is a Latin word that means "one-third of a foot." The species, *borealis*, comes from a Greek word that means "northern."

Purple Pitcher-plant

Sarracenia purpurea ORDER **Ericales**
HEIGHT **8–16 in (20.3–40.6 cm)** ⋅ HABITAT **Bogs and wetlands** ⋅ RANGE **Most of eastern United States; Washington, California, and Alaska; throughout Canada** ⋅ ZONES **6 to 8** ⋅ TYPE **Perennial** ⋅ **Eudicot**

Each spring, the Purple Pitcher-plant produces one flower at the top of a curving, leafless stalk. The flower has five rounded, reddish purple petals. Insects must walk inside the flower to reach the pollen and nectar. Luckily for them, this part of the wildflower is safe. The leaves are another story. A ring of bronzy, reddish green leaves grows at the plant's base. The leaves are hollow and flare out around the top. Inside, they are lined with downward pointing hairs. When it rains, the leaves fill with water. And when insects enter the leaves, they're trapped. They drown in the water. Bacteria and enzymes in the water digest the insects, and the Purple Pitcher-plant absorbs the nutrients.

REDDISH PURPLE FLOWER WITH FIVE ROUNDED PETALS

CURVING, LEAFLESS STALK

WILDFLOWER watcher!

The larvae of at least two insects—a mosquito and a midge—live inside Purple Pitcher-plant leaves. Nobody knows why the enzymes in the water don't digest the larvae. The enzymes do digest the larvae of other mosquito species.

10s spotters

Laugh Out Loud!

Why did the coach fire the Purple Pitcher-plant?

All it wanted to do was catch.

California Pitcher-plant

Darlingtonia californica ORDER **Ericales** ◦ HEIGHT **8–24 in (20.3–61 cm)** ◦ HABITAT **Seeps, meadows, bogs, and fens** ◦ RANGE **California, Oregon, and Washington in the U.S.; British Columbia, Canada** ◦ ZONES **7 to 10** ◦ TYPE **Perennial** ◦ **Eudicot**

The California Pitcher-plant, also called the Cobra Lily, has modified leaves that grow into tall, twisted tubes. The leaves are yellowish green but turn reddish purple toward the top. At the top, the leaves widen and fold down like a hood. Two structures resembling a mustache or a fishtail hang beneath the hood. There's also a round opening here that gives insects access to the nectar inside. Most insects visit the plant, collect nectar, and leave. But those that fall to the bottom of the tube become trapped. The tube is lined with downward pointing hairs that keep the insects from crawling out. And the leaves produce and release water. Insects drown in the pool of water and are digested by bacteria.

True **or** False

There's a state park dedicated to protecting the California Pitcher-plant.
True. Darlingtonia State Natural Site is a botanical park in Oregon. It was created to protect this threatened species.

REDDISH PURPLE FLOWER WITH FIVE ROUNDED PETALS

CURVING, LEAFLESS STALK

WILDFLOWER *watcher!*

Downward-pointing hairs aren't the only things keeping insects inside the California Pitcher-plant's tube. The inside of the hood has a waxy surface. Insects can't get a grip, so they slide down. And some parts of the hood are translucent. These "windows" confuse insects and keep them from finding the real exit.

DEEP PINK, BOWL-SHAPED FLOWERS

10s spotters

LEAVES: DARK GREEN AND HAIRLESS ON TOP BUT GRAY AND HAIRY UNDERNEATH

DANGER! ☠

Eating any part of an Alpine Laurel plant can be a fatal mistake. All members of the *Kalmia* genus are toxic.

Alpine Laurel

Kalmia microphylla ◦ ORDER **Ericales** ◦ HEIGHT **8–20 in (20.3–50.8 cm)** ◦ HABITAT **Bogs and wet mountain meadows** ◦ RANGE **Western United States, most of Canada, and Alaska** ◦ ZONES **3 to 9** ◦ TYPE **Perennial** ◦ Eudicot

Alpine Laurel is a low-growing, matted plant. Its deep pink flowers grow near the tops of leafy stems. Each flower has five petals and the petals take the shape of a shallow bowl. There are 10 notches in this bowl. The stamens insert their anther tips into these pockets. As the flower matures, the stamens grow longer and begin to bow. The tension on the stamen increases. Finally, an insect lands on the flower. The stamen is triggered, and the anther springs loose. It showers the insect with pollen. If you want to see the spring in action, you can trigger it with a toothpick or pencil.

....

Trailing Arbutus

WAXY WHITE OR PINK TRUMPET-SHAPED FLOWERS

10s spotters

STIFF, LEATHERY, DEEP GREEN LEAVES

NAME GAME

Trailing Arbutus was the first flower the Pilgrims saw after their first difficult winter in North America. Because of that, this wildflower is also called the Plymouth Mayflower.

Epigaea repens ◦ ORDER **Ericales** ◦ HEIGHT **4–6 in (10.2–15.2 cm)** ◦ HABITAT **Sandy or rocky acidic soil in woodlands or clearings** ◦ RANGE **Eastern United States and southeastern Canada** ◦ ZONES **3 to 9** ◦ TYPE **Perennial** ◦ Eudicot

Trailing Arbutus is a rare evergreen plant that forms a mat along the ground. Spotting this species can be difficult. That's because it tends to grow under fallen leaves. Trailing Arbutus has stiff, leathery, deep green leaves. Clusters of flowers grow at the ends of its hairy stems. The flowers are waxy and trumpet-shaped and can be white or pink. They have a fragrant, spicy scent, though you might need to lie down right next to the flowers to get a whiff. After the flowers die back, little white berries appear.

Spotted Wintergreen

WAXY WHITE OR PINK FLOWERS WITH BROWN SPOTS

REDDISH BROWN TWIGLIKE STEM

Chimaphila maculata ORDER Ericales ▪ HEIGHT 6–12 in (15.2– 30.5 cm) ▪ HABITAT Dry woods ▪ RANGE Eastern United States and Arizona, southeastern Canada ▪ ZONES 5 to 8 ▪ TYPE Perennial ▪ Eudicot

The Spotted Wintergreen's reddish brown stem looks like a slender twig. A spiral of thick, leathery leaves grows at the bottom of the stem. The leaves are spear-shaped and come to a sharp point at the tip. Their most notable characteristic is their coloring. The veins in these green leaves are white. And in winter, the leaves turn purple. Small

GREEN, SPEAR-SHAPED LEAVES WITH WHITE VEINS

flowers bloom at the end of the stem between June and August. The flowers have five waxy white or pink petals with brown spots. Ten tan stamens, shaped somewhat like clothespins, surround the large green pistil. The plant has sometimes been used to flavor candy and root beer.

Liverleaf Wintergreen

Pyrola asarifolia ORDER Ericales ▪ HEIGHT 6–12 in (15.2– 30.5 cm) ▪ HABITAT Moist woods, lakeshores, bogs, and wetlands ▪ RANGE Northern and western United States; throughout Canada; Alaska ▪ ZONES 3 to 9 ▪ TYPE Perennial ▪ Eudicot

WHITE OR PINK FLOWERS WITH DARKER PINK OR PURPLE EDGES

GREEN, HEART-SHAPED LEAVES WITH LONG PETIOLES

Liverleaf Wintergreen is an evergreen, creeping perennial. It has a simple, straight stem. A few heart-shaped leaves with long petioles grow in a ring at the base of the stem. The leaves are shiny, dark green, and leathery. Loose clusters of downward-facing flowers grow at the top of the stem. Each flower has five round white or pink petals with darker pink or purple edges. The 10 stamens have dark pink or red anthers at their tips. The long, light green style hangs from the middle of the flower like an elephant's trunk.

WILDFLOWER watcher!

Wintergreen leaves contain a natural painkiller. They can be chewed or used to create a dressing for wounds. Native Americans used the leaves to treat everything from sore eyes to kidney pain.

Laugh Out Loud!

What did the wildflower general say to his troops?

"Stamen, until I give the signal to move ahead!"

WILDFLOWER REPORT
WEIRD FLOWERS

Longbranch Frostweed

Sap oozes out from cracks in a Longbranch Frostweed's (see page 72) stem. Ice crystals form as the sap freezes.

THE FLOWERS OF A SKUNK CABBAGE CAN HEAT THEMSELVES UP TO A TOASTY 59°F (15°C). THEY MELT THE SNOW AND ICE AROUND THE PLANT IN EARLY SPRING.

SOME WILDFLOWERS ARE KNOWN FOR THEIR BEAUTY.

Others are recognized as noxious weeds. Some have parts you can eat. And others contain deadly poisons. There are many different kinds of wildflowers. And they have many different kinds of traits. It's not surprising that some of them, like the ones shown here, can only be described as weird.

Flatleaf Bladderwort

Only the flower of a Flatleaf Bladderwort (see page 121) grows above the water. And it's a trap. It snaps shut when insects land. Then it digests them.

Queen of the Prairie

When the Queen of the Prairie (see page 83) blooms, it looks like pink cotton candy.

Fiddleneck

The tip of a Fiddleneck's (see page 113) stem is shaped just like the neck of a fiddle!

Showy Prairie Gentian

Eustoma exaltatum ORDER **Gentianales** • HEIGHT **1–3 ft (0.3–0.9 m)**
• HABITAT **Moist fields and prairies; along streams** • RANGE **Central United States
from Texas to Montana** • ZONES **8 to 10** • TYPE **Annual/Biennial/Perennial** • Eudicot

The Showy Prairie Gentian is one of the most
eye-catching wildflowers in its habitat. Its tall,
straight stem and oval leaves are blue-green. The
flowers grow on long stalks from short branches
at the top of the plant. These bell-shaped flowers
grow up to two inches (5 cm) across. They face
upright and their petals flare out from the flower's deep throat. The petals are pale purple or
blue, fade to white, and become darker purple at
the base. The stamens are green, but the large
anthers at their tips are bright yellow.

LARGE, BELL-SHAPED FLOWERS

**→ LOOK FOR THIS
WHEN THE SHOWY PRAIRIE
GENTIAN** first opens, the pol-
len-laden anthers are the only yellow
parts in its throat. The green stigma
finally opens after all of the pollen
has been released. Then it splits into
two big yellow lobes.

Harvestbells

NARROW, SPEAR-SHAPED LEAVES

Gentiana saponaria ORDER **Gentianales**
• HEIGHT **8–20 in (20.3–50.8 cm)** • HABITAT **Moist
meadows, wooded slopes, and damp roadside
ditches** • RANGE **Southern and eastern United
States** • ZONES **4 to 7** • TYPE **Perennial** • Eudicot

Harvestbells, also known as
the Soapwort Gentian, have
a smooth, slender, light green
or reddish central stem. Narrow,
spear-shaped leaves grow
opposite each other up the stem.
At the top, up to six flowers

**PALE VIOLET-BLUE,
VASE-SHAPED
FLOWERS**

**SMOOTH, SLENDER,
LIGHT GREEN
OR REDDISH
CENTRAL STEM**

WILDFLOWER *watcher!*

Bumblebees are the
Harvestbells' primary pollinator,
but getting that job done can
be quite difficult. Sometimes,
the bumblebees have to fight
their way down the narrow
opening to reach the nectar
inside. Other times, they just
chew through the flower.

can grow in a cluster. The flowers are pale violet-blue. Often, they have
purple, white, or green streaks running up their sides. Harvestbells
bloom between August and October. But even when in full bloom, this
vase-shaped wildflower barely opens. Lighter-colored membranes run
between the flower's five lobes. Only the top can separate.

Rocky Mountain Fringed Gentian

Gentianopsis thermalis ORDER **Gentianales**
• HEIGHT **Up to 14 inches (35.6 cm)** • HABITAT **Meadows, bogs, and moist ground** • RANGE **Western United States** • ZONES **3 to 7** • TYPE **Annual** • Eudicot

PURPLE FLOWERS
WITH FOUR PETALS

SPEAR-SHAPED LEAVES
AT BASE OF STEM

The Rocky Mountain Fringed Gentian grows as a clump of stems. Each stem has two to four spear-shaped leaves at its base. In late summer, one flower blooms at the top of each stem. The flowers are up to three inches (7.6 cm) long. Each flower has four deep blue petals. The petals have fringed edges and they overlap. On sunny days, the petals lie back. This creates a square-shaped opening in the middle that gives pollinators easy access to the reproductive parts. On cloudy days, the flower closes. The petals pull together so they look like the blades on a windmill. The Rocky Mountain Fringed Gentian is the official flower of Yellowstone National Park.

Monument Plant

Frasera speciosa ORDER **Gentianales**
• HEIGHT **5–7 ft (1.5–2.1 m)** • HABITAT **Rich soil in woodland openings at moderate to high elevations** • RANGE **Western United States** • ZONES **3 to 5** • TYPE **Perennial** • Eudicot

WILDFLOWER watcher!

Monument Plants can live for up to 80 years. How tall the flower stalks grow depends on the altitude where the plants grow. In the alpine tundra, above the tree line, flower stalks average 18 inches (45.7 cm) tall, but they can be as short as 9 inches (22.9 cm). At the lower elevations, stalks are about 5 feet (1.5 m) tall, but can grow as tall as 9 feet (2.7 m)!

WIDE-OPEN, STAR-
SHAPED, WHITE FLOWERS
WITH GREEN STREAKS
AND PURPLE DOTS

The Monument Plant is a common wildflower that grows scattered across mountain meadows. It has a tall stalk that towers above a ring of long, narrow, pale green leaves at the plant's base. This wildflower is a monocarpic plant, meaning it lives for many years, but it only flowers once and then dies. When it does bloom, it goes all out. Thousands of plants may flower at the same time in mass-flowering events that happen at two- to seven-year intervals. Each plant produces up to 600 flowers. The wide-open, star-shaped flowers are white with green streaks and purple dots.

Fringed Bluestar

Amsonia ciliata ORDER **Gentianales** HEIGHT **2–3 ft (0.6–0.9 m)** HABITAT **Dry, open woodlands and sandy hills** RANGE **Southern United States** ZONES **5 to 9** TYPE **Perennial** Eudicot

PALE BLUE FLOWERS WITH FIVE PETALS

Laugh Out Loud!

Why does the Fringed Bluestar think it's famous?

Its flowers look like stars.

When the Fringed Bluestar emerges as a new plant, it has tiny hairs on its leaves and stem. This "fringe" is how the plant gets its common name. The Fringed Bluestar is a mid to late spring–blooming wildflower that grows in bushy clumps. The stem of each plant is lined with narrow, needle-like leaves. The leaves are soft and smooth and have one vein running down their middle. Each leaf attaches directly to the stem. A cluster of star-shaped flowers blooms at the top. Each flower has five petal-like lobes. The flowers are pale blue and have a white ring in their centers. In late fall, long after the flowers are gone, the leaves and stems turn yellow.

Spreading Dogbane

Apocynum androsaemifolium ORDER **Gentianales** HEIGHT **1.5–3 ft (0.5–0.9 m)** HABITAT **Forests, woodlands, prairies, meadows, rocky bluffs, and sandy fields** RANGE **Throughout most of the United States and Canada** ZONES **3 to 10** TYPE **Perennial** Eudicot

BRANCHING LIGHT GREEN TO RED STEM

PINK FLOWERS WITH DARK PINK STRIPES INSIDE

True **or** False

The Spreading Dogbane is related to milkweeds.
True. All Dogbanes are related to milkweeds. And both the leaves and stems of the Spreading Dogbane contain a milky juice.

The Spreading Dogbane is a native perennial found in most of North America. Its smooth, cylindrical stems vary in color from light green to red. Lined with four-inch (10.2 cm)-long oval leaves, the stems branch out in all directions. This gives the wildflower a bushy appearance. Clusters of two to ten fragrant, bell-shaped flowers grow at the ends of stems and leaf branches. The flowers have five pink lobes with dark pink stripes inside. They curl back at the tips.

Common Milkweed

CLUSTERS OF TINY PURPLE FLOWERS

LONG, OVAL LEAVES WITH A THICK, RED VEIN DOWN THE MIDDLE

Asclepias syriaca ORDER **Gentianales** • HEIGHT **2–6 ft (0.6–1.8 m)** • HABITAT **Disturbed areas in pastures and fields, oil fields, thickets, and along fencerows and railroad tracks** • RANGE **Eastern half of the United States; Montana and Oregon; southeastern Canada** • ZONES **3 to 9** • TYPE **Perennial** • Eudicot

The Common Milkweed has a stout, light green stem. Its big, oval leaves are dark green on top, light green on the bottom, and have a thick, red vein in the middle. A toxic, milky juice oozes out if either the leaves or stem are cut.

STOUT, LIGHT GREEN STEM

Monarch Butterflies lay their eggs on Common Milkweeds. This flower's leaves are the only thing Monarch caterpillars eat. From June to August, this wildflower produces big, round clusters filled with up to 100 tiny purple flowers. After the flowers wilt, thick, gray seedpods develop. They are covered with short woolly hair and soft spikes. When the seedpods split open, seeds with large tufts of white hair blow away in the wind.

FLAT CLUSTERS OF ORANGE, YELLOW, OR RED FLOWERS

Butterfly Weed

Asclepias tuberosa ORDER **Gentianales** • HEIGHT **1–2.5 ft (0.3–0.8 m)** • HABITAT **Prairies, open woodlands, canyons, and hillsides** • RANGE **Eastern and southern United States** • ZONES **3 to 9** • TYPE **Perennial** • Eudicot

The Butterfly Weed has hairy stems and stiff, narrow, spear-shaped leaves. Unlike other species in its family, this wildflower's stems aren't filled with a milky sap. But the green leaves and stems do make it easy for the plant's brightly colored flowers to stand out. The Butterfly

HAIRY STEMS

STIFF, NARROW, SPEAR-SHAPED LEAVES

Weed's flowers grow in a flat cluster at the top of the plant. They are usually orange, but they can also be yellow or red. The flowers, which bloom between May and September, are a favorite source of nectar for butterflies and hummingbirds.

> **→ LOOK FOR THIS**
> **BUTTERFLY WEED** flowers have five sepals and five petals. The petals, also called corolla lobes, point downward. This hides the sepals from view. Five hoods, which look like small petals, point up. They form a corona, or crown, at the top of the flower. Slender horns and the flower's reproductive parts are located inside the corona.

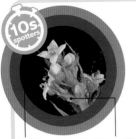

SMALL CLUSTERS OF TINY WHITE FLOWERS

THIN, OBLONG LEAVES COVERED WITH DOWNWARD-FACING HOOKS

Stickywilly

Galium aparine ORDER Gentianales · HEIGHT 1–3 ft (0.3–0.9 m) · HABITAT Moist woodlands, meadows, fields, and thickets · RANGE Throughout the United States and southern Canada; Alaska · ZONES 4 to 8 · TYPE Annual · Eudicot

Stickywilly is a weak-stemmed climbing plant. It has downward-facing hooks on its stems and leaves. This allows it to climb up nearby plants for support. The hooks will also grab onto your pants, socks, and shoelaces if you brush against them. Stickywilly grows from a shallow, branching taproot. Its stem is square and weak. Its thin, oblong leaves grow in spirals of six to eight along the stem. Small clusters of tiny white flowers grow at stems that rise from the leaf axils.

WILDFLOWER watcher!

Although it is technically a wildflower, Stickywilly is generally classified as a weed. In some Canadian provinces, it's listed as a noxious weed.

Azure Bluet

Houstonia caerulea ORDER Gentianales · HEIGHT 3–8 in (7.6–20.3 cm) · HABITAT Moist ledges, low prairies, sandy banks, sandy open forests, and glades · RANGE Eastern United States and southeastern Canada · ZONES 3 to 8 · TYPE Perennial · Eudicot

WILDFLOWER watcher!

Azure Bluet produces two different types of flowers. Some flowers have long stamens and a short style. Others have short stamens and a long style. It's difficult to see the difference with the naked eye. In both types of flowers, the reproductive parts are inserted in the corolla tube. This phenomenon, called "heterostyly," occurs in many plant families, and is a way of encouraging cross-pollination.

Azure Bluets are also called Quaker Ladies because of their shy, modest appearance. This wildflower is a small, dainty perennial that blooms between April and July. A ring of spatula-shaped leaves grows at the bottom of its slender, square, light green stem. A few small, darker green leaves grow opposite each other up the stem. One or two small flowers bloom at the top of each stem. Each flower has four pale violet-blue petal-like lobes and a yellow center. The lobes are shaped like eggs, but they're pointed at the tip.

PALE VIOLET-BLUE FLOWERS WITH YELLOW CENTERS

LONG, HAIRY STEM THAT CURLS LIKE A FIDDLE NECK AT THE TIP

YELLOW-ORANGE FLOWERS
ON THE CURLED TIP

Fiddleneck

Amsinckia menziesii ORDER **Boraginales** • HEIGHT **2–4 ft (0.6–1.2 m)**
• HABITAT **Grasslands, pastures, and roadsides** • RANGE **Western and northeastern
United States, western Canada, and Alaska** • ZONES **3 to 8** • TYPE **Annual** • Eudicot

Anyone who's seen a fiddle will immediately
understand how the Fiddleneck got its name.
The tip of the stem curls around, just like the
neck of a fiddle! Other than that curl, the
Fiddleneck has a long, straight stem. Spear-shaped
leaves up to six inches (15.2) long alternate their way
up the stem. The leaves and the stem are hairy. Some of the hairs
are long and bristly. Others are short and point down. The plant's
yellow-orange flowers grow on the curl at its tip.

Hoary Puccoon

Lithospermum canescens
ORDER **Boraginales** • HEIGHT **6–18 in
(15.2–45.7 cm)** • HABITAT **Dry prairies,
open woodlands, and along roads and
railroads** • RANGE **Eastern United States
and southeastern Canada** • ZONES **2 to 8**
• TYPE **Perennial** • Eudicot

CLUSTERS OF BRIGHT
YELLOW-ORANGE,
TUBULAR FLOWERS
AT THE TIPS OF
THE STEMS

The Hoary Puccoon is a common
wildflower in eastern North America. It can
be easy to spot when its bright yellow-orange
flowers bloom in early spring. The Hoary Puccoon
produces multiple stems from the same root
system. The stems are straight at the bottom but may
branch out on top. Small, narrow, spear-shaped
leaves alternate their way up the stems. Both
the leaves and the stems are covered with
silky hairs. The tube-shaped flowers have five
rounded petal-like lobes.

NAME GAME

The Hoary Puccoon is very
hairy. So why isn't it called the
Hairy Puccoon instead? One
definition of the word "hoary"
is "white with age." Another is
"covered with fine white hairs."
It's actually a very fitting name
for this wildflower.

Laugh Out Loud!

What kind of wildflower
has a big family?

One with deep roots.

LIGHT GREEN, CYLINDRICAL CENTRAL STEM

DROOPING CLUSTERS OF BLUE BELL-SHAPED FLOWERS

→ **LOOK FOR THIS**
VIRGINIA BLUEBELLS flowers are about an inch (2.5 cm) long. The corolla of each flower is made up of five shallow lobes. Inside the corolla are five white stamens with light brown anthers and one long, slender, white style.

Virginia Bluebells

Mertensia virginica ORDER **Boraginales** ▪ HEIGHT **1–2.5 ft (0.3–0.8 m)** ▪ HABITAT **Moist woodlands and clearings; river floodplains** ▪ RANGE **Eastern United States and southeastern Canada** ▪ ZONES **3 to 8** ▪ TYPE **Perennial** ▪ Eudicot

The Virginia Bluebells plant has a smooth, cylindrical central stem. Its big oval leaves are soft and floppy. They alternate their way up the stem. Hanging clusters of pink buds appear in early spring. The buds open to reveal delicate, bell-shaped flowers. Newly opened flowers have a pinkish tint. But as the flowers mature they turn blue. Virginia Bluebells' blooms last for about three weeks. When the flowers are gone, the fruits develop. Each fruit contains four dark brown, wrinkled nutlets. These are the wildflower's seeds.

Tall Fringed Bluebells

Mertensia ciliata ORDER **Boraginales**
▪ HEIGHT **1–3 ft (0.3–0.9 m)** ▪ HABITAT **Stream banks, wet meadows, and damp thickets** ▪ RANGE **Western United States** ▪ ZONES **4 to 8** ▪ TYPE **Perennial** ▪ Eudicot

Tall Fringed Bluebells is the tallest type of Bluebells plant. It is often seen growing in large patches next to small mountain streams. This wildflower's thick, stout stem branches out on top. Long, oval leaves with pointed tips crowd the stem. The blue-green leaves are covered with a waxy coating and have small hairs along their edges. Hanging clusters of fragrant, narrow, bell-shaped flowers bloom from June to August. The flower buds are pink. After the flowers open, they turn blue. But as the flowers age, they become pink once again.

CLUSTERS OF NARROW, BELL-SHAPED BLUE FLOWERS

THICK, STOUT STEM THAT BRANCHES OUT AT TOP

SPEAR-SHAPED, BLUE-GREEN LEAVES WITH A WAXY COATING AND SMALL HAIRS ALONG THE EDGES

True **or** False

Another common name for Tall Fringed Bluebells is Mountain Bluebells.
True. This wildflower grows at medium to high mountain elevations.

Plants in the *Mertensia* genus are also called "Lungworts."
True. That's because they resemble a different species in Europe. People thought that plant could cure lung disease.

Eastern Waterleaf

Hydrophyllum virginianum ORDER **Boraginales** ▪ HEIGHT **1–2 ft (0.3–0.6 m)** ▪ HABITAT **Moist woodlands, stream valleys, and floodplains** ▪ RANGE **Eastern United States and southeastern Canada** ▪ ZONES **4 to 8** ▪ TYPE **Perennial** ▪ Eudicot

The Eastern Waterleaf's leaves are sharply divided into three to five leaflets. The leaflets have jagged edges. But their most remarkable characteristic is their coloring. The first leaves that appear in early spring are splotched with white patches. This makes the green leaves look like they have been stained by spilled water. The lavender flowers bloom from May and June. They grow in round clusters with up to 20 tiny flowers each. The flowers are bell-shaped, and they have long, narrow sepals with feathery edges.

CLUSTERS OF TINY LAVENDER, BELL-SHAPED FLOWERS WITH FEATHERY SEPALS

→ LOOK FOR THIS
THE STAMENS in an Eastern Waterleaf flower are quite noticeable. They have hairy, white filaments and yellow anthers that turn brown as the flower ages. They also stick out well beyond the flower's petals.

Silky Phacelia

CLUSTERS OF DEEP PURPLE, BELL-SHAPED FLOWERS

LONG BLUISH PURPLE STAMENS WITH YELLOW ANTHERS

Phacelia sericea ORDER **Boraginales** ▪ HEIGHT **4–16 in (10.2–40.6 cm)** ▪ HABITAT **Open, rocky areas at mid to high mountain elevations** ▪ RANGE **Western United States, southwestern Canada, and Alaska** ▪ ZONES **5 to 10** ▪ TYPE **Biennial/Perennial** ▪ Eudicot

The Silky Phacelia's deep purple flowers are shaped like tiny bells. Their extra-long stamens are bluish purple and have bright yellow tips.

WILDFLOWER *watcher!*

If you're out searching for gold, you might want to keep an eye out for Silky Phacelia. This plant absorbs gold from the soil into its tissues when it grows. A large colony of this species might indicate that there's gold down below!

They stick out so far that they make the flowers look fuzzy. The Silky Phacelia's flowers grow in a thick cluster at the top of a straight, woody stem. The cluster uncoils and straightens as the plant matures. Most of this wildflower's leaves grow at the bottom of the stem. The fernlike leaves are covered with so many silky hairs that they look silver.

WHITE, LAVENDER, OR PINK
FUNNEL-SHAPED FLOWERS

Hedge False Bindweed

Calystegia sepium ORDER **Solanales** ∘ HEIGHT **Up to 10 ft (3.1 m)**
∘ HABITAT **Moist prairies, thickets, woodlands, and fields; along streams, road-
sides, railroads, and fencerows** ∘ RANGE **Throughout the United States, southern
Canada, and Alaska** ∘ ZONES **3 to 9** ∘ TYPE **Perennial** ∘ Eudicot

Hedge False Bindweed is a nonnative perennial
vine. It climbs up other plants and objects and
wraps its slender, green stem around them for
support. Although this vine can grow quite long,
its arrowhead-shaped leaves are spaced far apart
on the stem. The funnel-shaped flowers grow
from leaf axils all along the stem. They can get up
to three inches (7.6 cm) wide and may be white,
lavender, or pink. Once a flower opens, it usually
only lives for one day.

DON'T BE FOOLED

**Many people confuse Hedge
False Bindweed** with Common
Morning-glory. To tell the difference, look at the flowers and the
leaves. Hedge False Bindweed has
white, pink, or lavender flowers
and arrowhead-shaped leaves.
Common Morning-glory flowers
are purple, blue, pink, white, or a
combination of those colors. And
its leaves are shaped like hearts.

Bush Morning-glory

Ipomoea leptophylla ORDER **Solanales**
∘ HEIGHT **1.5–3 ft (0.5–0.9 m)** ∘ HABITAT **Dry
prairies, meadows, roadsides, and dunes**
∘ RANGE **Central United States from Texas to Montana**
∘ ZONES **4 to 10** ∘ TYPE **Perennial** ∘ Eudicot

WILDFLOWER watcher!

Bush Morning-glory does well
in droughts because of its root
system. Its lateral roots can
branch out 15 to 25 feet (4.6 to
7.6 m). Its taproot can grow up
to 24 inches (61 cm) wide and
four feet (1.2 m) long.

The Bush Morning-glory has long,
narrow, spear-shaped leaves.
Unlike many other Morning-glory
species, it isn't a vine. Instead, it

PINKISH PURPLE OR
PURPLISH RED FUNNEL-
SHAPED FLOWERS

has lots of stems that branch out to form a bushy
clump. This wildflower produces clusters with one
to three large funnel-shaped flowers. The flowers
are pinkish lavender or purplish red. The throat is
the darkest part of each flower. Bush Morning-
glory flowers bloom between June and August.
Like other Morning-glories, its flowers are only
open in the morning and close in the afternoon.

Sacred Thorn-apple

BIG, WHITE, FUNNEL-SHAPED FLOWERS

Datura wrightii ORDER **Solanales** • HEIGHT **2–4 ft (0.6–1.2 m)**
• HABITAT **Sandy or gravelly dry, open slopes; next to gardens, roads, and railroads**
• RANGE **Most of the United States** • ZONES **9 to 11** • TYPE **Annual/Perennial** • Eudicot

The Sacred Thorn-apple is a large wildflower found in most parts of the U.S. The plant grows up to four feet (1.2 m). And its coarse, gray stems branch out up to six feet (1.8 m) wide. Large, egg-shaped leaves alternate their way along the stems. The white, funnel-shaped flowers bloom from May to November. Like the rest of the plant, they're big. They can grow up to eight inches (20.3 cm) long and six inches (15.2 cm) wide. The flowers open in the evening and close by mid-morning the next day.

DANGER!

The Sacred Thorn-apple is one wildflower you definitely do not want to eat. The entire plant, particularly the seeds, is highly toxic.

BRANCHING, SPINE-COVERED STEMS

Buffalobur Nightshade

Solanum rostratum ORDER **Solanales**
• HEIGHT **Up to 2 ft (0.6 m)** • HABITAT **Pastures, yards, rocky open ground, moist fields, roadsides, and next to railroads** • RANGE **Throughout the United States and southern Canada** • ZONES **3 to 9** • TYPE **Annual** • Eudicot

CLUSTERS OF FLAT, ROUND, YELLOW FLOWERS

By all accounts, Buffalobur Nightshade is a nuisance. The entire plant, except the petals, is covered with sharp, stiff spines. The spines discourage livestock from eating this toxic plant. But they sure do hurt if you touch them! Buffalobur Nightshade grows from a thick taproot. Prickly green leaves with rounded lobes grow on its branching stems. Bright yellow flowers grow in clusters. The flowers are flat, round, and about an inch (2.5 cm) across. Five stamens, one much longer than the others, stick out from the middle of the flower.

WILDFLOWER watcher!

Buffalobur Nightshade's fruits are round burs covered with long, sharp spines. These burs easily catch on animal fur. Long ago, the seeds were transported when they latched onto the long, shaggy coats of American bison (buffalo).

SPOTTED WATER HEMLOCK IS THE MOST DEADLY PLANT IN NORTH AMERICA. EVERY PART OF THE PLANT IS POISONOUS.

BEAUTY CAN BE DECEIVING. Some wildflowers provide important medicines, but others can make you sick when you eat them or touch them. Some even contain deadly poisons that can kill you. It's not always easy to figure out which plants are dangerous and which ones aren't. Many deadly plants look a lot like other plants that you eat and enjoy every day. You should never eat a plant unless you know for sure what it is. That's why it's important to learn about the wildflowers around you. Watch out for these flowers.

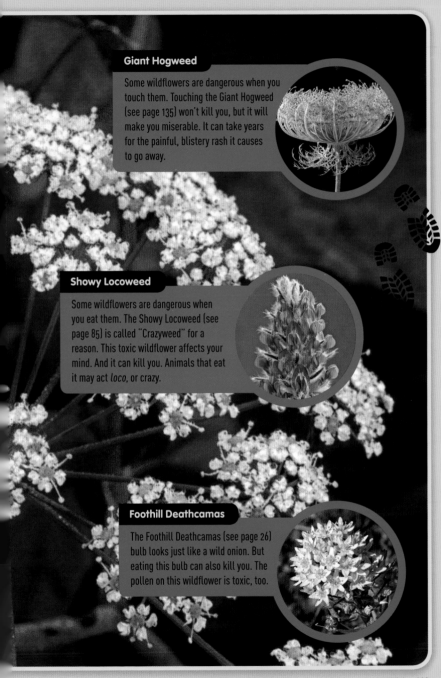

Giant Hogweed

Some wildflowers are dangerous when you touch them. Touching the Giant Hogweed (see page 135) won't kill you, but it will make you miserable. It can take years for the painful, blistery rash it causes to go away.

Showy Locoweed

Some wildflowers are dangerous when you eat them. The Showy Locoweed (see page 85) is called "Crazyweed" for a reason. This toxic wildflower affects your mind. And it can kill you. Animals that eat it may act *loco*, or crazy.

Foothill Deathcamas

The Foothill Deathcamas (see page 26) bulb looks just like a wild onion. But eating this bulb can also kill you. The pollen on this wildflower is toxic, too.

Carolina Wild Petunia

Ruellia caroliniensis ORDER **Lamiales** • HEIGHT **12–18 in (30.5–45.7 cm)** • HABITAT **Sandy uplands, woodlands, and clearings** • RANGE **Southern and eastern United States** • ZONES **5 to 10** • TYPE **Perennial** • Eudicot

The Carolina Wild Petunia is one of the first wildflowers to bloom in the spring. Its tough, woody root system allows it to bounce back quickly from the winter cold. It continues to bloom until early fall. Often the flowers bloom in pairs. But they stay open for only one day. The Carolina Wild Petunia has a multibranched stem. Oval leaves grow opposite each other up the stem. Its trumpet-shaped flowers have five widely spread lobes. The flowers are about an inch (2.5 cm) across and are bluish purple in color. They have long, pointed calyx lobes at their base. Their nectar attracts butterflies, honeybees, wasps, and hummingbirds.

WILDFLOWER watcher!

The Carolina Wild Petunia's petals look like those of true petunias. But the two species aren't related. True petunias belong to the Solanaceae family. The Carolina Wild Petunia is a member of Acanthaceae, which includes many tropical and sub-tropical wildflower species.

BLUISH PURPLE, TRUMPET-SHAPED FLOWERS

OVAL LEAVES

Flatleaf Bladderwort

YELLOW, SNAPDRAGON-SHAPED FLOWER WITH RED STRIPES

SLENDER STEMS

Utricularia intermedia ORDER **Lamiales** · HEIGHT **4–10 in (10.2–25.4 cm)** · HABITAT **Shallow ponds, slow-moving streams, and wet meadows** · RANGE **Northern and western United States, throughout Canada, and Alaska** · ZONES **3 to 8** · TYPE **Annual** · Eudicot

Flatleaf Bladderwort is a deceiving wildflower. Most of its parts grow underwater. Unless you look below the surface, you won't see how its slender stems creep along the bottom. Nor will you see the flat, branching leaves. But you will see the flower. It grows above water, and it's a trap—at least for small insects. The flower is bright yellow, has red stripes, and is shaped like the flower on a snapdragon. When something brushes against it, it quickly springs open and shut. Both water and prey rush into a little sac called a "bladder." Enzymes inside the bladder digest the intruder.

Laugh Out Loud!

How is a Flatleaf Bladderwort like a teenager?

They both like fast food.

Blueflower Butterwort

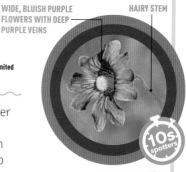

WIDE, BLUISH PURPLE FLOWERS WITH DEEP PURPLE VEINS

HAIRY STEM

Pinguicula caerulea ORDER **Lamiales** · HEIGHT **2–6 in (5–15.2 cm)** · HABITAT **Sandy, moist pinelands, bogs, and ditches** · RANGE **Southeastern United States** · ZONES **8 to 10** · TYPE **Perennial** · Eudicot

Like its cousins the Bladderworts, Blueflower Butterwort is a carnivore. But it doesn't devour prey with its flowers. It does so with its leaves. Blueflower Butterwort has a clump of shiny, yellowish green leaves. The leaves are covered with short hairs. And these hairs produce a substance that's really sticky. When an insect lands on the leaves, it gets stuck. Then, the edges of the leaf roll over. The leaf doesn't completely close, but it does get to work digesting the insect. Once the insect is completely dissolved, the leaf flattens out again.

WILDFLOWER watcher!

The pattern of veins on Blueflower Butterwort flowers acts as a road-map to the nectar. The veins lead bees to nectar found deep inside the flower's throat. This also ensures that the bees brush up against the flower's reproductive parts to collect and distribute pollen.

CLUSTERS OF TUBE-SHAPED, ROSY PINK FLOWERS

Rose Vervain

Glandularia canadensis ORDER **Lamiales** HEIGHT **6–24 in (15.2–61 cm)**
- HABITAT **Prairies, plains, woodlands, bluffs, pastures, and alongside roads and railroads**
- RANGE **Eastern two-thirds of the United States** ZONES **6 to 9** TYPE **Perennial** Eudicot

SPEAR-SHAPED LEAVES WITH
THREE DEEPLY DIVIDED LOBES

Rose Vervain is a long-blooming, creeping wild-flower with hairy stems. Its spear-shaped leaves are deeply divided into three lobes. They may also be hairy. This wildflower can spread to form large mats over the course of a summer. Dome-shaped clusters of rosy pink, tube-shaped flowers bloom at its branch tips. The flowers have five petals and four stamens. The filaments are white and the anthers are green. Rose Vervain grows well in sandy or rocky soil. But it needs lots of sun. This wildflower doesn't grow well in the shade.

HAIRY SPIKES OF PINK OR PURPLE FLOWERS

Hoary Verbena

Verbena stricta ORDER **Lamiales** HEIGHT **1–4 ft (0.3–1.2 m)**
- HABITAT **Fields and prairies** RANGE **Most of the United States; southeastern Canada**
- ZONES **3 to 9** TYPE **Annual/Perennial** Eudicot

LIGHT GREEN TO DULL
RED, HAIRY STEM
BIG, OVAL, HAIRY LEAVES
WITH JAGGED EDGES

The Hoary Verbena is a tall, hairy wildflower. It has long, white hairs on its stem. The hairs on its leaves are finer. But they're thick enough to make the undersides of the leaves look white. There are even hairs on the tall flower spike at the top of the plant. The spikes on a Hoary Verbena plant can be up to eight inches (20.3 cm) long. They are packed with pink or purple flowers. The flowers bloom one or two at a time. The bottom of the spike blooms first.

WILDFLOWER watcher!

These plants are rarely on the menu for mammals. The foliage is hairy, and it tastes bitter. Ranchers who find Hoary Verbena in their pastures usually consider it a weed.

Laugh Out Loud!

What do you tell wildflowers when they disagree?

"Leaf it alone."

Scarlet Beebalm

Monarda didyma ORDER **Lamiales** ◦ HEIGHT **2–3 ft (0.6–0.9 m)**
◦ HABITAT **Moist, open woodlands; thickets, meadows, and stream banks**
◦ RANGE **Eastern and Pacific Northwest in United States; southeastern Canada**
◦ ZONES **4 to 9** ◦ TYPE **Perennial** ◦ Eudicot

FLOWER HEADS WITH A RING OF RED, TUBULAR FLOWERS

The Scarlet Beebalm's central stem is square and slightly hairy. Its spear-shaped leaves are slightly hairy, too. But if you see this wildflower, it might take you a moment to notice these hairy parts. Your eyes will be focused on the flower heads. Each flower head is about four inches (10.2 cm) wide. It contains a ring of red, tubular flowers. Just below the flowers are several red or purple leaf bracts. These flowers start blooming in late June. All of the flowers in a ring bloom at the same time.

→ **LOOK FOR THIS**
SCARLET BEEBALM flowers have no smell. But the wildflower's leaves smell like mint. The stem of this plant, and others in the mint family, is square. You can feel the shape with your fingers!

Hoary Skullcap

CLUSTERS OF SMALL PURPLISH BLUE FLOWERS

FOUR-SIDED CENTRAL STEM

Scutellaria incana ORDER **Lamiales** ◦ HEIGHT **2–3 ft (0.6–0.9 m)** ◦ HABITAT **Upland forests, rocky woodlands and slopes, thickets, and roadsides** ◦ RANGE **Eastern United States** ◦ ZONES **5 to 8** ◦ TYPE **Perennial** ◦ Eudicot

Hoary Skullcap is a branched perennial with a four-sided central stem. Fine hairs make the green stem look white. Oval leaves with jagged edges grow opposite each other up the stem. The leaves are yellowish green on top. Fine, white hairs make them look whitish green underneath. Clusters of small purplish blue flowers grow at the end of each stem. The tube-shaped flowers have two lips. The upper lip is shaped like a hood. Its sides curl back. The lower lip is larger, broader, and has a patch of white in the flower's throat.

NAME GAME

There are about 300 species in the *Scutellaria* genus. These flowers get their common name from the shape of the calyx at the base of the flowers. It is shaped like a tiny medieval helmet, which was called a "skullcap."

Scarlet Monkeyflower

Mimulus cardinalis ORDER **Lamiales** HEIGHT **2–3 ft (0.6–0.9 m)**
 HABITAT **Stream banks, bogs, wet meadows, and seeps** RANGE **Western United States** ZONES **6 to 9** TYPE **Perennial** Eudicot

Hummingbirds and hawk moths absolutely love the Scarlet Monkeyflower. They are attracted to the perennial's large reddish orange flowers and are rewarded with nectar. The flowers, while tubular, have an unusual shape. The upper petals bend forward. The lower petals bend backward. The stamens and pistil arch downward and stick out prominently in the middle. This ensures that hummingbirds brush against these parts when they come to get the nectar. Scarlet Monkeyflower's spear-shaped leaves are light green and hairy. Glands on the leaves secrete a sticky substance.

LARGE, REDDISH ORANGE FLOWERS

→ LOOK FOR THIS
THE SCARLET MONKEYFLOWER is a big, bushy plant. Each plant grows about three feet high (0.9 m) and just as wide. Mature plants have several stems. As the stems age, they start to look floppy.

Foxglove Beardtongue

Penstemon digitalis ORDER **Lamiales** HEIGHT **2–5 ft (0.6–1.5 m)**
 HABITAT **Low, moist prairies; open woodlands; fields** RANGE **Eastern United States and southeastern Canada** ZONES **3 to 8** TYPE **Annual/Perennial** Eudicot

Foxglove Beardtongue survives the winter as a cluster of broad, oval leaves. The leaves are medium green and have red tints. When spring arrives, one or more tall, flowering stalks begin to grow from that leaf base. Shiny, spear-shaped leaves grow up the stalks. By late spring or early summer, pairs of white flowers bloom in a cluster at the top of each stem. Each tubular flower is about an inch (2.5 cm) long. Sometimes there are little purple lines inside the flower. The lines show visiting bees where they can find the nectar.

PAIRS OF WHITE FLOWERS GROWING IN A CLUSTER AT THE TOP OF EACH STEM

NAME GAME

Foxglove Beardtongue's scientific name comes from the Greek words *pente* ("five") and *stemon* ("stamen") and the Latin word *digitus* ("finger"). This name makes sense because this plant's flowers look like the fingers of a glove.

Entireleaf Indian Paintbrush

Castilleja indivisa ORDER **Lamiales** ∘ HEIGHT **6–16 in (15.2–40.6 cm)** ∘ HABITAT **Sandy pastures, woodland edges, and roadsides** ∘ RANGE **Texas, Oklahoma, Arkansas, and Louisiana** ∘ ZONES **5 to 9** ∘ TYPE **Annual** ∘ Eudicot

The Entireleaf Indian Paintbrush is an upright annual wildflower. It grows in large patches, particularly in sandy pastures. This wildflower has a straight, hairy stem and long, thin, spear-shaped leaves. It looks like it has a cluster of red flowers growing at the top of its stem. But if you look closely, you'll see that only part of the flowers is red. These one-inch (2.5-cm)-long flowers are mostly white and green. Only the tips of the flowers are red. The tips of the leaf bracts growing beneath the flowers are red, too. The flowers and leaf bracts look like paintbrushes dipped in red paint.

WILDFLOWER watcher!

The Entireleaf Indian Paintbrush is a parasitic plant. Its roots attach to the roots of other plants. Then the plant gets some of the nutrients it needs to grow from the other plant.

SMALL WHITE-AND-GREEN FLOWERS WITH RED TIPS

10s spotters

LEAF BRACTS WITH RED TIPS IN THE FLOWER CLUSTER

STRAIGHT, HAIRY STEM

LONG, THIN, SPEAR-SHAPED LEAVES

Laugh Out Loud! What do you call a plant that feeds off another plant?

Hungry.

Sitka Valerian

Valeriana sitchensis ORDER **Dipsacales** ▪ HEIGHT **1–4 ft (0.3–1.2 m)** ▪ HABITAT **Moist meadows and woodlands at mid to high elevations** ▪ RANGE **Western United States, western Canada, and Alaska** ▪ ZONES **3 to 8** ▪ TYPE **Annual** ▪ Eudicot

Many wildflowers grow better out in the open. But not the Sitka Valerian. When protected by trees and other taller vegetation, it can grow up to four feet (1.2 m) tall. In open meadows, it's lucky to reach a foot (0.3 m). The Sitka Valerian is a common wildflower found all the way from California to Alaska. This perennial grows from a stringy underground root system. Two to five pairs of leaves grow opposite each other up the smooth stem. The leaves are divided into three to five leaflets and they have wavy edges. Up to 20 tiny white to pink flowers grow in a dense, rounded cluster at the top of the stem. The flowers are tube-shaped and have five lobes and three long stamens. After the flowers die back, the fruits develop. Each fruit produces one tiny, hairy seed.

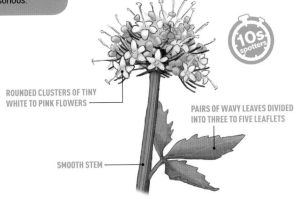

ROUNDED CLUSTERS OF TINY WHITE TO PINK FLOWERS

PAIRS OF WAVY LEAVES DIVIDED INTO THREE TO FIVE LEAFLETS

SMOOTH STEM

Harebell

Campanula rotundifolia ORDER **Asterales** • HEIGHT **12–20 in (30.5–50.8 cm)** • HABITAT **Meadows, grasslands, rocky slopes, alpine areas, and sandy shores** • RANGE **Most of the United States, throughout Canada, and Alaska** • ZONES **3 to 6** • TYPE **Annual** • Eudicot

The Harebell is a highly adaptable wildflower. It grows in full sun and shade and in a wide range of habitats. It grows throughout the United States—except for the Southeast. Heat is one thing this wildflower cannot tolerate. A Harebell grows from a ring of small, rounded, long-stalked leaves. Narrow, linear leaves alternate their way up the wildflower's thin, wiry stems. The thin, papery flowers are blue-violet and shaped like bells. Just one downward-facing flower may bloom at the end of each stem or the flowers may appear in groups of two to three. After the flowers die back, oval seed capsules grow. Each capsule is filled with lots of tiny seeds.

NAME GAME

One possible reason for the Harebell's common name is quite logical. The wildflower grows in places with lots of hares (close relatives of rabbits). Another reason is a bit more of a folktale. Some people believed that witches squeezed juices from the flower. Then they used the juices to transform themselves magically into hares.

True or False

Harebells grow in Scotland.
True. This hardy little wildflower grows all over the world. In Scotland, its flowers were once used to create the blue dye for tartans.

Many different animals eat Harebell leaves.
False. The leaves at the bottom of the stem wither away before the flower blooms. The stem leaves are too small for animals to notice.

10s spotters

THIN, WIRY STEMS

BLUE-VIOLET, BELL-SHAPED FLOWERS

NARROW, LINEAR STEM LEAVES

SPIKE OF BRIGHT RED FLOWERS

→ **LOOK FOR THIS**
YOU WON'T SEE many insects pollinating Cardinal Flowers. It's too difficult for them to get down inside these long, tubular flowers. But keep your eyes peeled for hummingbirds. They pollinate the flowers when they feed on the nectar.

SPIKE OF BLUE-VIOLET FLOWERS

TALL, ROUND CENTRAL STEM

WILDFLOWER watcher!

Most animals don't eat the leaves of the Great Blue Lobelia. They produce a toxic substance that causes ailments from nausea to convulsions. The one exception is deer. Scientists speculate that deer might have a stronger immunity to the toxins.

Cardinal Flower

Lobelia cardinalis ORDER **Asterales** ◦ HEIGHT **2–4 ft (0.6–1.2 m)** ◦ HABITAT **Moist areas, including stream banks, roadsides, prairies, near lakes or ponds, and swamps** ◦ RANGE **All but northwestern United States; southeastern Canada** ◦ ZONES **3 to 9** ◦ TYPE **Perennial** ◦ Eudicot

The Cardinal Flower is a clump-forming perennial. The lower half of its unbranched stem is green. That's where the spear-shaped leaves grow. In late summer, the top half turns red. That's when the eight-inch (20.3-cm) spike of flowers blooms. Each flower in the spike has five petals. There are two petals on top and three spreading out wide on the bottom. The petals join together in a long, slender tube. The wildflower's common name comes from these flowers. They resemble the bright red robes that Roman Catholic cardinals wear.

Great Blue Lobelia

Lobelia siphilitica ORDER **Asterales** ◦ HEIGHT **2–3 ft (0.6–0.9 m)** ◦ HABITAT **Open, wet woodlands; stream banks; marshes; and meadows** ◦ RANGE **Eastern two-thirds of the United States; southeastern Canada** ◦ ZONES **4 to 9** ◦ TYPE **Perennial** ◦ Eudicot

The Great Blue Lobelia has a tall, usually unbranched central stem. The round stem is generally smooth, but it can be a little bit hairy sometimes. Long, wide, oval leaves alternate their way up the stem. The top of the stem features a spike of flowers that can be up to two feet (0.6 m) long. The flowers in the spike are blue-violet and have white patches near the throat. Each flower has five petals. The two slender petals on top bend backward. The three oval petals on the bottom hang down. The flowers bloom for about two months, beginning in late summer.

Common Yarrow

FLAT, DENSE FLOWER HEADS WITH YELLOWISH WHITE FLOWERS

LACY, FERNLIKE LEAVES

Achillea millefolium ORDER **Asterales** ◦ HEIGHT **2–3 ft (0.6–0.9 m)**
◦ HABITAT **Roadsides, fields, waste areas, and lawns** ◦ RANGE **Throughout the United States and Canada** ◦ ZONES **3 to 9** ◦ TYPE **Perennial** ◦ Eudicot

Common Yarrow has a tall, upright stem that only branches out near the top. Its leaves look like delicate, lacy ferns. They smell spicy. The flowers appear in dense, flat flower heads at the top of each stem. Each flower head has up to 25 yellowish white flowers and can be up to four inches (10.2 cm) across. Although this wildflower is found throughout North America, it is not a native species. Common Yarrow was introduced long ago from Europe and Asia. It can form dense mats as it spreads. In many places, it is considered to be a weed.

TALL, UPRIGHT STEM THAT BRANCHES AT THE TOP

NAME GAME

Common Yarrow gets its scientific name *Achillea millefolium*, from Greek mythology. Achilles was the hero of the Trojan War. In the myths, he used this plant to heal his soldiers' wounds on the battlefield. This wildflower is, in fact, known for its ability to slow and stop the flow of blood.

Hairy White Oldfield Aster

Symphyotrichum pilosum ORDER **Asterales** ◦ HEIGHT **Up to 3.5 ft (1.1 m)**
◦ HABITAT **Prairies, meadows, woodlands, vacant lots, rocky cliffs, and alongside roads and railroads** ◦ RANGE **Eastern United States; southeastern and southwestern Canada** ◦ ZONES **5 to 8** ◦ TYPE **Perennial** ◦ Eudicot

CLUSTERS OF LITTLE WHITE FLOWERS WITH YELLOW CENTERS

The Hairy White Oldfield Aster can grow and spread so much that this wildflower looks more like a shrub. Its branching stems are light green and covered with scattered hairs. As the plant ages, lower stems become red and lose their hairs. Spear-shaped leaves alternate their way up the stem. And the upper stems each end with a cluster of flowers. Each three-quarter-inch (1.9-cm) flower in the cluster has up to 35 tiny petals around a yellow center. Scaly bracts surround the flower's base.

Laugh Out Loud!

What's it called when wildflowers fill a flowerbed?

A bedspread.

Indian Blanket

Gaillardia pulchella ORDER Asterales · HEIGHT 1–2 ft (0.3–0.6 m) ·
HABITAT Roadsides, drainage ditches, and open fields · RANGE All but
northwestern United States; southeastern Canada; Alaska and
Hawaii · ZONES 3 to 11 · TYPE Annual/Biennial/Perennial · Eudicot

When the Indian Blanket first
emerges in spring, it's just a ring
of hairy, multilobed leaves. But
then the ring expands and a long
stem starts to grow. Hairy leaves
with jagged edges grow on the stem.
Lower leaves are spear-shaped. Upper
leaves are shaped like a spatula. The leaves
get smaller as they rise up the stem. The
flower grows on a long, slender stalk at the
top of the stem. It is divided into a ring of
ray florets, or smaller flower parts. Each floret has three petals that are fused together
at the base. Most often, the flower has a
brownish red center and orange-red petals
with yellow tips.

WILDFLOWER *watcher!*

The Indian Blanket, also called
Firewheel, grows well in sunny,
sandy, well-drained locations.
The plants don't fare as well if
they are planted in rich soils.
They produce fewer flowers, and
the plants are big and droopy.

→ LOOK FOR THIS
INDIAN BLANKET pet-
als are usually reddish
purple or orange-red with
yellow tips. But they can
also be solid orange, yellow, pink, or white. The
center of the flower disk
can be brownish red, red-
dish purple, orange-red,
or yellow.

RED FLOWERS WITH YELLOW OUTER RIM

10s spotters

Black-eyed Susan

Rudbeckia hirta ORDER **Asterales** ▪ HEIGHT **2–3 ft (0.6–0.9 m)**
▪ HABITAT **Prairies, plains, meadows, pastures, and woodland openings**
▪ RANGE **Throughout most of the United States, southern Canada, and Alaska**
▪ ZONES **3 to 7** ▪ TYPE **Annual/Biennial/Perennial** ▪ Eudicot

The Black-eyed Susan is found in most parts of the United States. It's well known, native, and easy to recognize. It has bright yellow, daisy-like flowers with dark brown centers. The flowers, which bloom from June to October, can be up to three inches (7.6 cm) wide. One flower grows at the tip of each stiff, hairy stem. Large, hairy, oval leaves alternate about halfway up the stem. The top is devoted to the flower. The center of each flower is actually a disk of dark brown florets. Together they form a flattened cone. Up to 20 bright yellow ray florets form a ring around the cone. Sometimes there's a maroon spot at the base of each ray floret.

WILDFLOWER watcher!

The Black-eyed Susan grows from seeds. Depending upon conditions, it may act as an annual, biennial, or perennial. If conditions are too perfect, it can reseed itself too much. But it won't take over. Older perennials in the area will keep the Black-eyed Susan population under control.

BRIGHT YELLOW, DAISY-LIKE FLOWERS WITH DARK BROWN CENTERS

LARGE, HAIRY, OVAL LEAVES

STIFF, HAIRY STEM

10s spotters

MAKE THIS!

Wildflower Art Project

1. Visit a museum or go online to view paintings of flowers.
2. Pick your favorite flower painting. Is the flower identified in the work's title? If not, use this guide or another source to identify it.
3. Research to learn more about the flower and the artist. Why do you think the artist chose to paint this flower? Analyze the style and mood.
4. Now create your own wildflower painting.

FLOWER HEAD WITH MANY BRIGHT YELLOW RAY FLORETS

HOLLOW, WHITE, LEAFLESS STEMS

Common Dandelion

Taraxacum officinale ORDER **Asterales** ▫ HEIGHT **6–24 in (15.2–61 cm)** ▫ HABITAT **Lawns, pastures, waste places, along roads and railroads** ▫ RANGE **Throughout North America** ▫ ZONES **3 to 10** ▫ TYPE **Perennial** ▫ **Eudicot**

It would be difficult to go an entire summer without seeing a Common Dandelion. This wildflower/weed is aggressive. It prefers moist areas with lots of sun. But it grows just about everywhere its seeds can take root. The Common Dandelion has a deep taproot. Its oblong, deeply cut leaves are clustered in a ring at the base of the plant. Flower heads, which close at night and on rainy days, bloom at the top of hollow, white, leafless stems. They contain many bright yellow ray florets. When the flower heads mature, they turn into a puffy, white ball of seeds.

NAME GAME

Common Dandelions are named for their leaves. The deeply cut edges of the leaves look like a lion's teeth. The common name comes from the French phrase *dent de lion*, which means "lion's tooth."

Common Sunflower

Helianthus annuus ORDER **Asterales** ▫ HEIGHT **3–10 ft (0.9–3.1 m)** ▫ HABITAT **Dry, open plains, prairies, meadows, and foothills** ▫ RANGE **Throughout North America** ▫ ZONES **2 to 11** ▫ TYPE **Annual** ▫ **Eudicot**

WILDFLOWER watcher!

There are many different hybrids of sunflowers. Each one has its own unique characteristics. For example, the flower heads on Common Sunflowers grow to about five inches (12.7 cm) wide. But the flower heads on mammoth varieties can be up to a foot (30.5 cm) across.

The Common Sunflower is a native plant that grows in dry, open areas. This wildflower can grow up to 10 feet (3.1 m) tall. It has a stiff, upright, hairy stalk and large, coarse leaves. A flower head grows at the end of each stem. Each flower head has a round center made up of brown disk flowers. A ring of bright yellow rays surrounds the disk. When the flowers mature, the disk flowers that are pollinated are replaced with sunflower seeds.

STIFF, UPRIGHT, HAIRY STALK

FLOWER HEADS WITH BROWN CENTERS SURROUNDED BY YELLOW RAYS

SPIKES OF DEEP PURPLE FLOWER HEADS

Dense Blazing Star

Liatris spicata ORDER **Asterales** ‣ HEIGHT **2–4 ft (0.6–1.2 m)** ‣ HABITAT **Moist, open woodlands, meadows, and marshes** ‣ RANGE **Eastern United States and southeastern Canada** ‣ ZONES **3 to 11** ‣ TYPE **Perennial** ‣ Eudicot

Unlike many other wildflowers in the Aster family, the Dense Blazing Star doesn't have any ray flowers. This tall, upright perennial's deep purple flower heads are made entirely of fluffy disk flowers. They bloom in a 6- to 12-inch (15.2–30.5-cm) spike at the top of the stem. Below the flower heads, the stems are quite leafy. A tuft of long, grass-like leaves grows at the bottom of the stem. Many more leaves alternate their way up the stem. There are so many leaves that it looks like they're growing in a spiral.

→ **LOOK FOR THIS**
THE DENSE BLAZING STAR blooms from July to September. Unlike most wildflowers, its flower heads don't bloom from the bottom up. They bloom from the top down.

Giant Goldenrod

LONG CLUSTERS OF TINY YELLOW FLOWER HEADS

Solidago gigantea ORDER **Asterales** ‣ HEIGHT **3–7 ft (0.9–2.1 m)** ‣ HABITAT **Woodland clearings; wet prairies and thickets; along rivers, ponds, and ditches** ‣ RANGE **Throughout most of North America** ‣ ZONES **3 to 8** ‣ TYPE **Annual** ‣ Eudicot

Giant Goldenrod is a tall perennial that has a light green or pale purple upright, central stem. The stem is lined with spear-shaped leaves that have sharp, jagged edges. The top of the stem branches out. Beginning in late summer, this is where the Giant Goldenrod earns its common name. Flowering leaf stalks grow at the top of the branching stems. Each stalk contains a long cluster of tiny yellow flower heads. The flowers bloom for about a month. After they wilt, they produce small, hairy seeds.

DON'T BE FOOLED
It's easy to confuse Giant Goldenrod with Canada Goldenrod. However, Giant Goldenrod grows in wet places and has a hairless stem. Canada Goldenrod grows in dry areas and has a hairy stem.

ASTERS (ASTERACEAE) **133**

Queen Anne's Lace

Daucus carota ORDER **Apiales** • HEIGHT **2–5 ft (0.6–1.5 m)** • HABITAT **Disturbed areas, pastures, fields, roadsides, and waste places** • RANGE **Throughout the United States and most of southern Canada** • ZONES **3 to 9** • TYPE **Biennial** • Eudicot

Queen Anne's Lace is an introduced species that is native to Eurasia and North Africa. It is found throughout most of North America. Although it has attractive flowers, in many places this biennial is considered to be a noxious weed. During the plant's first year, Queen Anne's Lace is just a ring of leaves growing from a large taproot. The second year, it takes off. Its slightly hairy, light green, hollow central stem shoots up to five feet (1.5 m) high. It branches out from the central stem. Feathery leaflets alternate their way up the stems. Then umbrella-shaped clusters packed with little white flowers bloom at the tips of the stems. Long, thin leaf bracts cup around the base of each cluster.

→ LOOK FOR THIS

AFTER QUEEN ANNE'S LACE flowers wilt, they produce flat, red, bristly fruits. Each fruit contains two seeds. Then, the umbrella-shaped clusters fold in on themselves. This traps the seeds inside. The clusters may be blown apart by the wind or fall off and roll like a tumbleweed. The fruits will also attach to an animal that brushes against the cluster.

DON'T BE FOOLED **Many members of the Carrot family** produce umbrella-shaped clusters of white flowers, so it's easy to get them confused. To identify Queen Anne's Lace accurately, look at the cluster. The central-most flower is usually dark purple. In some studies, this purple flower has been shown to attract pollinators. Scientists think the pollinators might mistake it for another insect when they are deciding whether to visit the plant.

UMBRELLA-SHAPED CLUSTERS OF LITTLE WHITE FLOWERS

FEATHERY LEAFLETS

10s spotters

Giant Hogweed

UMBRELLA-SHAPED CLUSTERS OF WHITE FLOWERS

Heracleum mantegazzianum ORDER **Apiales** ▪ HEIGHT **10–15 ft (3.1–4.6 m)** ▪ HABITAT **Yards, ravines, parks, abandoned lots, stream banks, woodlands, and roadsides** ▪ RANGE **Eastern and northwestern United States and Canada** ▪ ZONES **3 to 9** ▪ TYPE **Perennial** ▪ Eudicot

Giant Hogweed was introduced to North America from Asia as an ornamental plant. This massive plant's single, hollow stem can be up to six inches (15.2 cm) wide at the bottom. The stem is covered with dark reddish purple raised spots and stiff hairs. Leaves grow up to 10 feet (3.1 m) long and 5.6 feet (1.7 m) wide. Upper leaves are slightly smaller. When the plant blooms, it produces four to six stem leaves. An umbrella-shaped cluster of white flower grows at the tip of each one. Each cluster is about 2.5 feet (0.8) wide.

HAIRY STEM WITH REDDISH PURPLE SPOTS

DANGER!

Never, ever touch a Giant Hogweed. The sap in the leaves and stems is highly toxic. It contains a substance that changes the cell structure in your skin. Even brushing up against the plant can cause a severe skin rash and blisters.

Spotted Water Hemlock

Cicuta maculata ORDER **Apiales** ▪ HEIGHT **3–6 ft (0.9–1.8 m)** ▪ HABITAT **Wet fields, moist thickets, fens, and swamps** ▪ RANGE **Throughout North America** ▪ ZONES **2 to 8** ▪ TYPE **Biennial/Perennial** ▪ Eudicot

Spotted Water Hemlock grows in wet places. Its hollow, stout, smooth stem branches out. It may be pale green, pink, or reddish purple and can have noticeable veins. Umbrella-shaped clusters of small, white flowers bloom at the tip of each stem. Each leaf is divided into two or three long, slender leaflets with jagged edges. One central vein ends at the tip of each leaflet. All other veins end at the notches between the jagged edges rather than at the points on the sides of the leaf. This arrangement is highly unusual for a plant.

LEAVES WITH THREE LONG, SLENDER LEAFLETS WITH JAGGED EDGES

UMBRELLA-SHAPED CLUSTERS OF SMALL, WHITE FLOWERS

DANGER!

Spotted Water Hemlock is the most toxic plant in North America. All parts of the plant are extremely poisonous.

WILDFLOWER REPORT
BUILDING BETTER HABITATS

Do Your Research

Decide what types of wildflowers you're going to use. Then pick your location wisely. Each plant has specific requirements for sunlight, moisture, and nutrients.

Wildflowers Do Not Disturb

MANY PEOPLE PLANT WILDFLOWER GARDENS because they like to look at the flowers. But there's a more important reason to do this. Wildflowers attract pollinators. The pollinators visit pretty flowers. But they also take care of tomatoes, peas, and other plants that grow food. To build a sustainable wildflower garden, it helps to keep these tips in mind.

Start Small

Remember that big isn't always necessary. Lots of small wildflower gardens can connect to create a corridor. That's important for migratory species like the Monarch Butterfly.

Plant Seeds or Seedlings

Select native species, but buy them at a nursery. Most wildflowers die if you try to transplant them from their native habitat.

A WILDFLOWER MEADOW IN MOUNT RAINIER NATIONAL PARK, WASHINGTON STATE, U.S.A.

State Flowers

FORGET-ME-NOT Alaska

EVERY U.S. STATE HAS AN OFFICIAL STATE FLOWER, many of which are wildflowers!

ALABAMA: Camellia *(Camellia japonica)*

ALASKA: Forget-me-not *(Myosotis alpestris subsp. asiatica)*

ARIZONA: Saguaro Cactus blossom *(Carnegia gigantea)*

ARKANSAS: Apple blossom *(Malus domestica)*

CALIFORNIA: California poppy *(Eschscholzia californica)*

COLORADO: Rocky Mountain columbine *(Aquilegia caerulea)*

CONNECTICUT: Mountain laurel *(Kalmia latifolia)*

DELAWARE: Peach blossom *(Prunus persica)*

DISTRICT OF COLUMBIA: American Beauty rose *(Rosa 'American Beauty')*

FLORIDA: Orange blossom *(Citrus sinensis)*

GEORGIA: Cherokee rose *(Rosa laevigata)*

HAWAII: Pua aloalo *(Hibiscus brackenridgei)*

IDAHO: Syringa mock orange *(Philadelphus lewisii)*

ILLINOIS: Purple violet *(Viola sororia)*

INDIANA: Peony *(Paeonia lactiflora)*

IOWA: Wild prairie rose *(Rosa arkansana)*

KANSAS: Sunflower *(Helianthus annuus)*

KENTUCKY: Goldenrod *(Solidago gigantea)*

LOUISIANA: Magnolia *(Magnolia grandiflora)*

MAINE: Eastern white pine tassel and cone *(Pinus strobus)*

MARYLAND: Black-eyed Susan *(Rudbeckia hirta)*

MASSACHUSETTS: Mayflower *(Epigaea repens)*

MICHIGAN: Apple blossom *(Malus domestica)*

MINNESOTA: Pink and white ladyslipper *(Cypripedium reginae)*

MISSISSIPPI: Magnolia *(Magnolia grandiflora)*

WILD PRAIRIE ROSE North Dakota

MISSOURI: Hawthorn *(Crataegus punctata)*

MONTANA: Bitterroot *(Lewisia rediviva)*

NEBRASKA: Goldenrod *(Solidago gigantea)*

NEVADA: Sagebrush *(Artemisia tridentata)*

NEW HAMPSHIRE: Purple lilac *(Syringa vulgaris)*

NEW JERSEY: Violet *(Viola sororia)*

NEW MEXICO: Yucca *(Yucca glauca)*

NEW YORK: Rose (genus *Rosa*)

NORTH CAROLINA: Flowering dogwood *(Cornus florida)*

NORTH DAKOTA: Wild prairie rose *(Rosa arkansana)*

OHIO: Scarlet carnation *(Dianthus caryophyllus)*

OKLAHOMA: Mistletoe *(Phoradendron leucarpum)*

OREGON: Oregon grape *(Berberis aquifolium)*

PENNSYLVANIA: Mountain laurel *(Kalmia latifolia)*

RHODE ISLAND: Violet *(Viola palmata)*

SOUTH CAROLINA: Yellow jessamine *(Gelsemium sempervirens)*

SOUTH DAKOTA: Pasque flower *(Anemone patens* var. *multifida)*

TENNESSEE: Iris *(Iris germanica)*

TEXAS: Texas bluebonnet *(Lupinus texensis* and other species)

UTAH: Sego lily *(Calochortus nuttallii)*

VERMONT: Red clover *(Trifolium pratense)*

VIRGINIA: Flowering dogwood *(Cornus florida)*

WASHINGTON: Coast rhododendron *(Rhododendron macrophyllum)*

WEST VIRGINIA: Rhododendron *(Rhododendron maximum)*

WISCONSIN: Wood violet *(Viola sororia)*

WYOMING: Indian paintbrush *(Castilleja linariifolia)*

WOOD VIOLET Wisconsin

Alpine Golden
Buckwheat 88

Appalachian Barren
Strawberry 82

Berlandier's Yellow
Flax 60

Black-eyed Susan 131

Buffalobur Nightshade 117

Common Dandelion 132

Common Evening
Primrose 63

Common St. John's Wort 56

Common Sunflower 132

Desert Poppy 42

Drummond's
Mountain-Avens 83

Dwarf Cinquefoil 81

Fiddleneck 113

Flatleaf Bladderwort 121

Fringed Loosestrife 100

Giant Goldenrod 133

Goosefoot Violet 59

Hoary Puccoon 113

Largeflower Bellwort 23

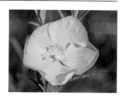
Longbranch Frostweed 72

Pale Touch-me-not 96

Silverweed 81

Skunk Cabbage 19

Slender Yellow
Wood Sorrel 53

Tinker's Penny 57

Western Tansymustard 77

Yellow Fritillary 22

Yellow Spiderflower 74

Yellow Trout Lily 21

Butterfly Weed 111

Cactus Apple 93

California Poppy 42

Common Jewelweed 96

Turk's-cap Lily 21

Western Wallflower 75

Alpine Laurel 104

Annual Phlox 98

Autumn Crocus 24

Bush Morning-glory 116

Carolina Wild Petunia 120

Common Blue Violet 58

Common Marshmallow 71

Common Milkweed 111

Copper Globemallow 70

Dark-throated Shooting Star 99

Dense Blazing Star 133

Dwarf Larkspur 49

Dwarf Sundew 89

Eastern Waterleaf 115

Fairy Slipper 30

Field Pansy 58

Fireweed 65

Hairy Clematis 48

Harvestbells 108

Hedge False Bindweed 116

Hoary Verbena 122

Jack-in-the-pulpit 18

Littleleaf Sensitive-briar 86

Liverleaf Wintergreen 105

Longbract Spiderwort 37

Narrowleaf Four O'clock 92

Old Man's Whiskers 80

Parry's Primrose 101

Pinkfairies 64

Pinkladies 63

Purple Loosestrife 67

Purple Milkvetch 85

Queen of the Prairie 83

Red Clover 84

Redstem Stork's Bill 61

Rocky Mountain Beeplant 73

Rocky Mountain Fringed Gentian 109

Rocky Mountain Iris 32

Rose Vervain 122

Roundleaf Orchid 31

Shoreline Seapurslane 91

Showy Locoweed 85

Showy Prairie Gentian 108

Sierra Fumewort 44

Silky Phacelia 115

Silvery Lupine 86

Smallflower Woodland-star 52

Spotted Geranium 61

Spreading Dogbane 110

Sticky Purple Geranium 62

Tapertip Onion 33

Threadleaf Sundew 89

Trailing Arbutus 104

Twolobe Larkspur 49

Water Hyacinth 36

Winged Lythrum 66

Cardinal Flower 128

Entireleaf Indian Paintbrush 125

Fire Pink 87

Indian Blanket 130

Purple Pitcher-plant 102

Red Columbine 50

Red Trillium 25

Scarlet Beebalm 123

Scarlet Gilia 97

Scarlet Monkeyflower 124

Azure Bluet 112

Blue-eyed Grass 32

Blueflower Butterwort 121

Fringed Bluestar 110

Great Blue Lobelia 128

Greek Valerian 98

Harebell 127

Hoary Skullcap 123

Pickerelweed 36

Prairie Flax 60

Prairie Spiderwort 37

Tall Fringed Bluebells 114

Virginia Bluebells 114

American
Lily-of-the-valley 35

American
Water-Plantain 17

Bloodroot 43

Bride's Feathers 80

Carolina Springbeauty 90

Common Arrowhead 16

Common Yarrow 129

Corn Lily 27

Crowpoison 33

Cutleaf Toothwort 75

Dutchman's Breeches 45

Early Saxifrage 51

Elegant Mariposa Lily 20

Foothill Deathcamas 26

Foxglove Beardtongue 124

Giant Hogweed 135

Hairy Rockcress 76

Hairy White Oldfield Aster 129

Halberdleaf Rosemallow 70

Heartleaf Foamflower 52

Lanceleaf Springbeauty 90

Large-flowered White Trillium 25

Mayapple 46

Monument Plant 109

Mountain Wood Sorrel 53

Nightblooming Cereus 93

Queen Anne's Lace 134

Sacred Thorn-apple 117

Sitka Valerian 126

Snowball Sand Verbena 92

Solomon's Plume 34

Spotted Water Hemlock 135

Spotted Wintergreen 105

Starflower 101

Stickywilly 112

Tall Thimbleweed 47

Twinleaf 46

Wild Strawberry 82

Yellow Mandarin 22

Broadfruit Bur-reed 39

Broadleaf Cattail 38

California Pitcher-plant 103

CREATE A BUTTERFLY GARDEN

1. Conduct research to identify butterfly species that are native to your area. Identify which butterfly species you'd like to attract.

2. Do more research to learn what types of flowers each of these butterfly species likes to visit. Be sure to include flowers that they like to feed on as well as flowers that they like to lay their eggs on for the caterpillars to eat.

3. Hit the books one more time to learn about the wildflowers. In what types of soil do they grow? How much sun and water do they need? At what time of day and year do they bloom? Keep in mind that you'll have better luck with your garden if you select native wildflower species.

4. Download pictures of each plant you decide to use. Use the photos to create a layout for your butterfly garden. Note that large patches of similar flowers are more likely to attract butterflies.

5. Select an appropriate site, get your plants, and start digging! If your research is correct, butterflies should start visiting as soon as the flowers start to bloom.

Glossary

ANGIOSPERM: Seed-producing, flowering plants

ANNUAL: Plant with a life cycle of no more than one year, and often much less

ANTHER: Part of the stamen that makes and stores pollen

AQUATIC: Having to do with water. An aquatic plant grows near or in water.

AXIL: The angle between a branch or leaf and the axis from which it grows

BIENNIAL: Plant with a life cycle of no more than two years

BLADDER: Small oval sacs on the underwater leaves of bladderwort plants that trap and digest prey

BULB: Underground storage organ of a plant with fleshy, energy-storing leaves at the top and a flat stem at the bottom

CALYX: The structure formed by sepals; typically encloses the corolla

COMMON NAME: Nonscientific name of a species, or what the organism is usually called

CONIFEROUS FOREST: A forest of trees with thin needles instead of flat leaves

COROLLA: The structure formed by petals, which often contains nectar at its base

EUDICOT: The most common type of angiosperms; characteristics include pollen with three pores, two cotyledons (first leaves), flowering parts in multiples of four or five, networks of leaf veins, and rings of veins in the stem

FILAMENT: Slender support holding the anther

GENUS: A biological classification ranking between the family and species; a group of organisms having one or more common characteristics

GERMINATE: To begin to grow

HERBACEOUS: Plants with non-woody stems that usually live for a single growing season

HYBRIDS: Plants created by cross-pollinating different kinds of plants

INVASIVE SPECIES: A type of plant or animal that is not indigenous to a particular area and causes economic or environmental harm

MONOCOT: A type of angiosperm; characteristics include pollen with one pore, one cotyledon (first leaf), flowering parts in multiples of three, parallel leaf veins, and scattered bundles of leaves in the stem

NOXIOUS: Physically harmful or destructive to living organisms; often used to describe invasive species

OVARY: Base of the pistil, containing one or more eggs

PEDICEL: Stalk bearing the flower

PERENNIAL: Plant with a life cycle of more than two years

PETAL: Individual segment of the corolla, typically colored

PETIOLE: A slender stem that supports the blade of a leaf

PISTIL: Female part of the flower

POLLINATION: Transfer of pollen from the male part of a plant to the female part of a plant

RAY FLORET: A small petal-shaped flower that extends out from the center of a flower head

RECEPTACLE: Enlarged area bearing flower organs

RUNNER: An elongated horizontal stem that grows from the base of a plant and can then develop roots to form a new plant

SCIENTIFIC NAME: The name, usually in Latin, of an organism's genus and species

SEED CAPSULE: The part of a fruit that holds the seeds

SEPAL: Individual segment of the calyx, usually green and leaflike

SILIQUE: The long, narrow seedpod of plants in the mustard family

SPECIES: Group of similar organisms that can reproduce with each other

STALK: Stem of a plant

STAMEN: Male part of a flower

STEM: Main stalk of a plant

STIGMA: Part of the pistil that receives pollen during pollination

STYLE: Connecting stalk between stigma and ovary

TAPROOT: The main root of a plant that grows straight down and has small roots growing out of its side

TEPAL: The combination of the petals and sepals found in some types of flowers where petals and sepals are difficult to separate

TOXIC: Poisonous

TUBER: Thick part of an underground stem of a plant, such as a potato, that stores energy

UMBEL: A rounded cluster of flowers that radiates out from the tip of the main stem

WILDFLOWER: Noncultivated angiosperm that grows in natural places without the help of people

HOARY VERBENA p. 122

WANT TO FIND OUT EVEN MORE
about wildflowers? Check out these books, websites, apps, and movie. Be sure to ask an adult to help you search the Web to find the sites below.

Books

Doty, Rebecca A. *A Children's Guide to Spring Wildflowers.* Quillworth Publishing, 2016.

Gardening for Butterflies: How You Can Attract and Protect Beautiful, Beneficial Insects. The Xerces Society, 2016.

Hood, Susan, and National Audubon Society. *Wildflowers (National Audubon Society First Field Guides).* Scholastic, 1998.

National Geographic Pocket Guide to Wildflowers of North America. National Geographic, 2014.

Wildflowers (National Geographic: My First Pocket Guide). National Geographic, 2002.

Websites

First Flower (NOVA/WGBH Educational Foundation): pbs.org/wgbh/nova/flower/

Plants Database (USDA): plants.usda.gov/java

The Private Life of Plants (BBC): bbc.co.uk/programmes/b01qbw1w

Wildflower Identification (Discover Life): discoverlife.org/mp/20q?guide =Wildflowers

Wildflowers, Ferns, & Trees of Colorado, New Mexico, Arizona & Utah (Rocky Mountain Biological Laboratory): swcoloradowildflowers.com

Apps

Audubon Wildflowers

FlowerChecker

NatureGate

PlantNet Plant Identification

Movie

Disneynature: *Wings of Life* (Rated G documentary)

Index

Boldface indicates illustrations.

Credits

AS = Alamy Stock Photo; DR = Dreamstime; GI = Getty Images; NGC = National Geographic Creative; SS = Shutterstock

Cover (background), Amygdala Imagery/Getty images; (explorer), Kevin Rechin; (UP RT), Beata Becla/Shutterstock; (CRT, pink), Steve Lagreca/Shutterstock; (CTR, purple), Tamara Kulikova/Shutterstock; (LO RT), Mark Herreid/Shutterstock; (Cactus), EuToch/Getty Images; (LO CTR LE), Jody Ann/Shutterstock; (back cover), Starover Sibiriak/Shutterstock; 1, addkm/SS; 2-3, Jason Kasumovic/SS; 4 (UP), Ed Reschke/GI; 4 (CTR), Alan Majchrowicz/GI; 4 (LO), Pixelarchitect/DR; 5, Pthawornwong/DR; 6, Arina P Habich/SS; 7 (UP), Natalia Aggiato/SS; 7 (LO), BlueRingMedia/SS; 9, NG Maps; 10 (UP), au989/SS; 10 (LO), Gail Jankus/Science Source; 11, Richard Thomas/DR; 12 (UP), Svetlana Ileva/SS; 14 (Background), Custom Life Science Images/AS; 15 (LO), Patrick Coin; 15 (UP), Deatonphotos/SS; 15 (CTR), Florapix/AS; 16 (UP), Robert Henno/AS; 16 (LO), Jenny Wang; 17 (UP), Keir Morse; 17 (LO), Forrest Jones; 18 (UP), All Canada Photos/AS; 18 (LO), Jenny Wang; 19 (UP), M. Andy/SS; 19 (LO), Jenny Wang; 20 (UP), Kevin Schafer/AS; 20 (LO), Forrest Jones; 21 (UP), Steffen Hauser/botanikfoto/AS; 21 (LO), Andrew Sabai/SS; 22 (UP), Christopher Burrows/AS; 22 (LO), Mindy Fawver/AS; 23 (UP), Dave Zubraski/AS; 23 (LO), Forrest Jones; 24 (UP), alexmak7/SS; 24 (LO), Forrest Jones; 25 (UP), Kyle Horner/SS; 25 (LO), Doug Vinez/SS; 26 (UP), Federica Grassi/GI; 26 (LO), Forrest Jones; 27 (UP), David W. Inouye; 27 (LO), Forrest Jones; 28-29 (Background), Panoramic Images/GI; 29 (UP), Natures Images/GI; 29 (CTR), Flowerphotos/GI; 29 (LO), David Inouye; 30 (UP), David Inouyne; 30 (LO), Forrest Jones; 31 (UP), Bob Gibbons/Science Photo Library; 31 (LO), Forrest Jones; 32 (UP), Evgeniymuhortov2/DR; 32 (LO), Rinuusbaak/DR; 33 (UP), George Grall/NGC; 33 (LO), Pinerivek/DR; 34 (UP), Martin Fowler/SS; 34 (LO), Jenny Wang; 35 (UP), illustrissima/SS; 35 (LO), Forrest Jones; 36 (UP), Ricardo de Paula Ferreira/SS; 36 (LO), Ricardo de Paula Ferreira/SS; 37 (UP), Nature and Science/AS; 37 (LO), Sari O'Neal/AS; 38 (UP), Daburke/DR; 38 (LO), Forrest Jones; 39 (UP), Nature and Science/AS; 39 (LO), Forrest Jones; 40-41 (Background), Kevin Knight/AS; 40 (LE), Roger Eritja/AS; 41 (UP), Rick & Nora Bowers/AS; 41 (CTR), Mike Read/AS; 41 (LO), Rolf Nussbaumer Photography/AS; 42 (UP), Svetlana Ileva/SS; 42 (LO), Christopher Talbot Frank/AS; 43 (UP), V. J. Matthew/SS; 43 (LO), Jenny Wang; 44 (UP), Robert Harding/AS; 44 (LO), Forrest Jones; 45 (UP), George Grall/GI; 45 (LO), Jenny Wang; 46 (UP), Susan Smith/EyeEm/GI; 46 (LO), Zoonar GmbH/AS; 47 (UP), Pixelarchitect/DR; 47 (LO), Forrest Jones; 48 (UP), Gordon Wiltsie/NGC; 48 (LO), Jenny Wang; 49 (UP), Adam Jones/GI; 49 (LO), James Hager/robertharding/GI; 50 (UP), David Inouye; 50 (LO), Jenny Wang; 51 (UP), Gail Jankus/GI; 51 (LO), Forrest Jones; 52 (UP), Michael Wheatley/AS; 52 (LO), Daniel Dempster Photography/AS; 53 (UP), Grant Heilman Photography/AS; 53 (LO), blickwinkel/AS; 54-55 (Background), SumikoPhoto/GI; 54 (CTR), Chris Burrows/GI; 55 (CTR), Rinusbaak/DR; 55 (LO), Kyle Horner/SS; 56 (UP), Gala_Kan/SS; 56 (LO), Jenny Wang; 57 (UP), Stephen Sharnoff; 57 (LO), Forrest Jones; 58 (UP), Kclarksphotography/DR; 58 (LO), Pthawornwong/DR; 59 (UP), David W. Inouye; 59 (LO), Forrest Jones; 60 (UP), Steve Shoup/SS; 60 (LO), Rick & Nora Bowers/AS; 61 (UP), Ken Wiedemann/GI; 61 (LO), Willypd/DR; 62 (UP), Alan L. Detrick/Science Source; 62 (LO), Forrest Jones; 63 (UP), Leerobin/DR; 63 (LO), FlowerPhotos/UIG via GI; 64 (UP), DM Larson/SS; 64 (LO), Forrest Jones; 65 (UP), David W. Inouye; 65 (LO), Jenny Wang; 66 (UP), Kevin Knight/AS; 66 (LO), Forrest Jones; 67 (UP), Grezova Olga/SS; 67 (LO), Jenny Wang; 68-69 (Background), Anton Kozyrev/SS; 69 (UP), ullstein bild/GI; 69 (CTR), Maxal Tamor/AS; 69, LesPalenik/SS; 70 (UP), Kenneth M Highfill/GI; 70 (LO), Shattil and Rozinski/Minden Pictures; 71 (UP), Christina Bollen/GI; 71 (LO), Forrest Jones; 72 (UP), Gail Jankus/Science Source; 72 (LO), Forrest Jones; 73 (UP), Martha Marks/SS; 73 (LO), Jenny Wang; 74 (UP), Jim West/AS; 74 (LO), Forrest Jones; 75 (UP), Mary Terriberry/SS; 75 (LO), Colleen Miniuk-Sperry/AS; 76 (UP), Buiten-Beeld/AS; 76 (LO), Forrest Jones; 77 (UP), David W. Inouye; 77 (LO), Forrest Jones; 78-79, haraldmuc/SS; 79 (UP RT), Maciej Olszewski/SS; 79 (UP LE), Chris Burrows/GI; 79 (LO RT), Ricardo de Paula Ferreira/SS; 79 (LO LE), Adam Jones/GI; 80 (UP), Penny Rogers Photography/GI; 80 (LO), Inger Anne Hulbækdal/SS; 81 (UP), Larrymetayer/DR; 81 (LO), Barnowlka/DR; 82 (UP), Plotnikov/DR; 82 (LO), Anoli50/DR; 83 (UP), Bob Gibbons/AS; 83 (LO), Brzostowska/SS; 84 (UP), Ivan Smuk/SS; 84 (LO), Jenny Wang; 85 (UP), AdamLongSculpture/GI; 85 (LO), James Hager/Robert Harding/GI; 86 (UP), James Hager/Robert Harding/GI; 86 (LO), Kevin Knight/AS; 87 (LO), Forrest Jones; 87 (UP), Adam Jones/GI; 88 (UP), RukiMedia/SS; 88 (LO), Forrest Jones; 89 (UP), Carol Dembinsky/Dembinsky Photo Associates/AS; 89 (LO), Fred Muller/Biosphoto; 90 (UP), Michael Wheatley/GI; 90 (LO), Randy Beacham/AS; 91 (UP), sutipong/SS; 91 (LO), Forrest Jones; 92 (UP), Photo Al Schneider, www.swcoloradowildflowers.com; 92 (LO), Nature and Science/AS; 93 (UP), KALin1980/SS; 93 (LO), Florian Andronache/SS; 94-95 (Background), Don Vail/AS; 94 (LE), Nature and Science/AS; 95 (UP), emkaplin/SS; 95 (CTR), Stan Osolinski/GI; 95 (LO), Panther Media GmbH/AS; 96 (UP), Kquinnferris/DR; 96 (LO), Al Petteway & Amy White/NGC; 97 (UP), cjchiker/SS; 97 (LO), Jenny Wang; 98 (UP), Ed Reschke/GI; 98 (LO), Maria Mosolova/GI; 99 (UP), David W. Inouye; 99 (LO), Jenny Wang; 100 (UP), Ottochka/SS; 100 (LO), Forrest Jones; 101 (UP), Don Grall/GI; 101 (LO), Egschiller/DR; 102 (UP), Karelgallas/DR; 102 (LO), Forrest Jones; 103 (UP), Ed Reschke/GI; 103 (LO), Forrest Jones; 104 (UP), Chris Cheadle/GI; 104 (LO), Ed Reschke/GI; 105 (UP), Michael P Gadomski/GI; 105 (LO), tbkmedia.de/AS; 106-107 (Background), Keiichi Takita/GI; 106 (LE), Science Source/GI; 107 (UP), Bob Gibbons/AS; 107 (CTR), Reinhard Bode/DR; 107 (LO), Martin Beebee/AS; 108 (UP), Bill Gozansky/AS; 108 (LO), Pure Stock/AS; 109 (UP), James Steinberg/Science Source; 109 (LO), Design Pics Inc/AS; 110 (UP), Jim and Lynne Weber/SS; 110 (LO), John W Bova/GI; 111 (UP), Kateryna A./SS; 111 (LO), Dea C. Delu/GI; 112 (UP), Nigel Cattlin/AS; 112 (LO), age fotostock/AS; 113 (UP), Robert Harding/AS; 113 (LO), Science Source/GI; 114 (UP), Mary Terriberry/SS; 114 (LO), George D Lepp/GI; 115 (UP), RukiMedia/SS; 115 (LO) James Steinberg/GI; 116 (UP), Fanwen/DR; 116 (LO), For Alan/AS; 117 (UP), Ingrid Curry/SS; 117 (LO), Steve Shoup/SS; 118-119 (Background), Gail Jankus/GI; 119 (UP), chert61/GI; 119 (CTR), James Hager/robertharding/GI; 119 (LO), Federica Grassi/GI; 120 (UP), TreesG Photography/SS; 121 (UP), Peter M. Dziuk/Minnesota Wildflowers; 121 (LO), Florida Images/AS; 122 (UP), Robert Henno/AS; 122 (LO), Mark Herreid/SS; 123 (UP), RukiMedia/SS; 123 (LO), Chris Burrows/GI; 124 (UP), Chris Burrows/GI; 124 (LO), Natures Images/GI; 125 (UP), Bill Heinsohn/AS; 125 (LO), Forrest Jones; 126 (UP), Nature and Science/AS; 126 (LO), Forrest Jones; 127 (UP), Mirvav/SS; 127 (LO), Jenny Wang; 128 (UP), kj2011/GI; 128 (LO), Chayaporn Suphavilai/SS; 129 (UP), Gala_kan/DR; 129 (LO), bkkm/GI; 130 (UP), addkm/SS; 130 (LO), Forrest Jones; 131 (UP), Maciej Olszewski/SS; 131 (LO), Jenny Wang; 132 (UP), Olga Denisova/SS; 132 (LO), Buffy1982/SS; 133 (UP), UGreen 3S/SS; 133 (LO), gubernat/SS; 134 (UP), Stephen Bonk/SS; 134 (LO), Jenny Wang; 135 (UP), Hgrose/DR; 135 (LO), Gail Jankus/Science Source; 136-137 (Background), Alan Majchrowicz/GI; 136 (LE), Chantal Ringuette/SS; 137 (UP), Danderson107/DR; 137 (CTR), tadamichi/SS; 138, HildaWeges Photography/SS; 139 (UP), Kenneth M Highfill/GI; 139 (LO), Imladris/SS; 140 (Buckwheat), NatPar Collection/AS; 140 (Strawberry), Anoli50/DR; 140 (Flax), Rick & Nora Bowers/AS; 140 (Susan), Maciej Olszewski/SS; 140 (Nightshade), Steve Shoup/SS; 140 (Dandelion), Olga Denisova/SS; 140 (Primrose), FlowerPhotos/UIG via GI; 140 (Wort), Gala_Kan/SS; 140 (Sunflower), Buffy1982/SS; 140 (Poppy), Christopher Talbot Frank/AS; 140 (Drummond's), Bob Gibbons/AS; 140 (Cinquefoil), Larrymetayer/DR; 140 (Fiddleneck), robertharding/AS; 140 (Bladderwort), Peter M. Dziuk/Minnesota Wildflowers; 141 (Loosestrife), Ottochka/SS; 141 (Goldenrod), gubernat/SS; 141 (Goosefoot), David W. Inouye; 141 (Puccoon), Science Source/GI; 141 (Bellwort), Dave Zubraski/AS; 141 (Frostweed), Gail Jankus/Science Source; 141 (Touch-me-not), Al Petteway & Amy White/NGC; 141 (Silverweed), Barnowlka/DR; 141 (Cabbage), NatureDiver/SS; 141 (Sorrel), blickwinkel/AS; 141 (Tinker's), Stephen Sharnoff; 141 (Tanseymustard), David W. Inouye; 141 (Fritillary), Christopher Burrows/AS; 141 (Spiderflower), Jim West/AS; 141 (Trout Lily), Steffen Hauser/botanikfoto/AS; 142 (Butterfly Weed), Dea C.Delu/GI; 142 (Cactus), KALin1980/SS; 142 (Poppy), Svetlana Ileva/SS; 142 (Jewelweed), Kquinnferris/DR; 142 (Lily), Andrew Sabai/SS;142 (Wallflower), Colleen Miniuk-Sperry/AS; 142 (Laurel), Chris Cheadle/GI; 142 (Phlox), Maria Mosolova/GI; 142 (Crocus), alexmak7/SS; 142 (Morning-glory), For Alan/AS; 142 (Petunia), TreesG Photography/SS; 142 (Violet), Kclarksphotography/DR; 142 (Marshmallow), Christina Bollen/GI; 142 (Milkweed), Kateryna A./SS; 142 (Globemallow), Shattil and Rozinski/Minden Pictures; 143 (Shooting Star), David W. Inouye; 143 (Blazing Star), UGreen 3S/SS; 143 (Larkspur), Adam Jones/GI; 143 (Sundew), Fred Muller/Biosphoto; 143 (Waterleaf), RukiMedia/SS; 143 (Slipper), David Inouyne; 143 (Pansy), Pthawornwong/DR; 143 (Fireweed), David W. Inouye; 143 (Clematis), Gordon Wiltsie/NGC; 143 (Harvestbells), PureStock/AS; 143 (Bindweed), Fanwen/DR; 143 (Verbena), Mark Herreid/SS; 143 (Jack-in-the-pulpit), Ed Reschke/GI; 143 (Sensitive-briar), Kevin Knight/AS; 143 (Liverleaf), tbkmedia.de/AS; 144 (Spiderwort), Nature and Science/AS; 144 (Narrowleaf), Photo Al Schneider, www.swcoloradowildflowers.com; 144 (Whiskers), Penny Rogers Photography/GI; 144 (Primrose), Don Grall/GI; 144 (Pinkfairies), DM Larson/SS; 144 (Pinkladies), Leerobin/DR; 144 (Loosestrife), Grezova Olga/SS; 144 (Milkvetch), AdamLongSculpture/GI; 144 (Queen), Brzostowska/SS; 144 (Clover), Ivan Smuk/SS; 144 (Redstem), Willypd/DR; 144 (Beeplant), Martha Marks/SS; 144 (Gentian), James Steinberg/Science Source; 144 (Iris), Rinus Baak/DR; 144 (Vervain), Robert Henno/AS; 145 (Orchid), Bob Gibbons/Science Photo Library; 145 (Seapurslane), sutipong/SS; 145 (Locoweed), James Hager/Robert Harding/GI; 145 (Gentian), Bill Gozansky/AS; 145 (Fumewort), Robert Harding/AS; 145 (Phacelia), James Steinberg/GI; 145 (Lupine), James Hager/Robert Harding/GI; 145 (Woodland-star), Michael Wheatley/AS; 145 (Geranium), KenWiedemann/GI; 145 (Dogbane), John W Bova/GI; 145 (Sticky Geranium), Alan L. Detrick/Science Source; 145 (Onion), Pinerivek/DR; 145 (Sundew), Carol Dembinsky/Dembinsky Photo Associates/AS; 145 (Arbutus), Ed Reschke/GI; 145 (Larkspur), James Hager/robertharding/GI; 146 (Hyacinth), Ricardo de Paula Ferreira/SS; 146 (Lythrum), Kevin Knight/AS; 146 (Cardinal), kj2011/GI; 146 (Paintbrush), Bill Heinsohn/AS; 146 (Fire Pink), Adam Jones/GI; 146 (Blanket), addkm/SS; 146 (Pitcher-plant), Karelgallas/DR; 146 (Columbine), David Inouye; 146 (Trillium), Kyle Horner/SS; 146 (Beebalm), RukiMedia/SS; 146 (Gilia), cjchiker/SS; 146 (Monkeyflower), Chris Burrows/GI; 147 (Bluet), age fotostock/AS; 147 (Grass), Evgeniymuhortov2/DR; 147 (Butterwort), Florida Images/AS; 147 (Bluestar), Jim and Lynne Weber/SS; 147 (Lobelia), Chayaporn Suphavilai/SS; 147 (Valerian), Ed Reschke/GI; 147 (Harebell), Mirvav/SS; 147 (Skullcap), Chris Burrows/GI; 147 (Pickerelweed), Ricardo de Paula Ferreira/SS; 147 (Flax), Steve Shoup/SS; 147 (Spiderwort), Sari O'Neal/AS; 147 (Tall Bluebells), George D Lepp/GI; 147 (Virginia Bluebells), Mary Terriberry/SS; 148 (Lily), illustrissima/SS; 148 (Plantain), Keir Morse; 148 (Bloodroot), V J Matthew/SS; 148 (Bride's), Inger Anne Hulbækdal/SS; 148 (Springbeauty), Michael Wheatley/GI; 148 (Arrowhead), Robert Henno/AS; 148 (Yarrow), Gala_kan/DR; 148 (Corn Lily), David W. Inouye; 148 (Crowpoison), George Grall/NGC; 148 (Toothwort), Mary Terriberry/SS; 148 (Breeches), George Grall/GI; 148 (Saxifrage), Gail Jankus/GI; 148 (Mariposa), Kevin Schafer/AS; 148 (Deathcamas), Federica Grassi/GI; 148 (Beardtongue), Ron Rowan Photography/SS; 149 (Hogweed), Hgrose/DR; 149 (Rockcress), Buiten-Beeld/AS; 149 (Oldfield), bkkm/GI; 149 (Rosemallow), Kenneth M Highfill/GI; 149 (Foamflower), Daniel Dempster Photography/AS; 149 (Springbeauty), Randy Beacham/AS; 149 (Trillium), Doug Vinez/SS; 149 (Mayapple), Susan Smith/EyeEm/GI; 149 (Monument), Mike Read/AS; 149 (Wood Sorrel), Grant Heilman Photography/AS; 149 (Cereus), Florian Andronache/SS; 149 (Lace), Stephen Bonk/SS; 149 (Thorn-apple), Ingrid Curry/SS; 149 (Valerian), Nature and Science/AS; 149 (Verbena), Nature and Science/AS; 150 (Plume), Martin Fowler/SS; 150 (Hemlock), Gail Jankus/Science Source; 150 (Wintergreen), Michael P Gadomski/GI; 150 (Starflower), Egschiller/DR; 150 (Stickywilly), Nigel Cattlin/AS; 150 (Thimbleweed), Pixelarchitect/DR; 150 (Twinleaf), Zoonar GmbH/AS; 150 (Strawberry), Plotnikov/DR; 150 (Mandarin), Mindy Fawver/AS; 150 (Bur-reed), Nature and Science/AS; 150 (Cattail), Daburke/DR; 150 (Pitcher-plant), Ed Reschke/GI; 151 (UP RT), Singkham/SS; 151 (LO RT), Serg64/SS; 151 (LO LE), Karen Grigoryan/SS; 152-153, Adam Jones/GI; 154, pryzmat/SS

Since 1888, the National Geographic Society has funded more than 12,000 research, exploration, and preservation projects around the world. The Society receives funds from National Geographic Partners, LLC, funded in part by your purchase. A portion of the proceeds from this book supports this vital work. To learn more, visit natgeo.com/info.

For more information, visit nationalgeographic.com, call 1-800-647-5463, or write to the following address:

National Geographic Partners
1145 17th Street N.W.
Washington, D.C. 20036-4688 U.S.A.

Visit us online at nationalgeographic.com/books

For librarians and teachers: ngchildrensbooks.org

More for kids from National Geographic: kids.nationalgeographic.com

For information about special discounts for bulk purchases, please contact National Geographic Books Special Sales: specialsales@natgeo.com

For rights or permissions inquiries, please contact National Geographic Books Subsidiary Rights: bookrights@natgeo.com

Designed by John Foster

Trade paperback ISBN: 978-1-4263-2995-1

Reinforced library binding ISBN: 978-1-4263- 2996-8

The plant hardiness zones of Canada on page 9 are reproduced with permission from Natural Resources Canada, Canadian Forest Service, 2017.

The publisher would like to thank Dr. David Inouye, professor emeritus, at the University of Maryland, College Park, for his guidance and knowledge. The publisher would also like to thank everyone who worked to make this book come together: Julie Agnone, project manager; Angela Modany, associate editor; Callie Broaddus, senior designer; Sarah J. Mock, senior photo editor; Debbie Gibbons and Mike McNey, map production; Forrest Jones, illustrator; Sean Philpotts, production director; Anne LeongSon and Gus Tello, design production assistants; Sally Abbey, managing editor; and Joan Gossett, editorial production manager.

Printed in China
17/RRDH/1